D1385366

You're ok, your dog's ok

You're ok, your dog's ok

MARCUS SCHNECK
AND
JILL CARAVAN

CHARTWELL
BOOKS, INC.

A QUINTET BOOK

Published by Chartwell Books
A Division of Book Sales, Inc.
110 Enterprise Avenue
Secaucus, New Jersey 07094

This edition produced for sale
in the U.S.A., its territories
and dependencies only.

ISBN 1-55521-817-2

This book was designed and produced by
Quintet Publishing Limited
6 Blundell Street
London N7 9BH

Creative Director: Richard Dewing
Designer: Ian Hunt
Project Editor: Laura Sandelson
Editor: Diana Vowles
Picture Researchers: Marcus Schneck and
Jill Caravan

Typeset in Great Britain by
Central Southern Typesetters, Eastbourne
Manufactured in Singapore by
Eray Scan Pte. Ltd.
Printed in Singapore by
Star Standard Industries Private Ltd.

DEDICATION:

To Snoopy, Princess, Smokey, Candy, Daisy,
Rose, Queen, Trail, Duke, Tiny, Peanuts, Blue-
Gyp, Gray-Gyp, Buttons and mostly Timber –
some of the dogs we have known and loved.

Contents

Introduction

What if dogs are really smarter than us and are actually behaving in certain ways just to amuse and astound us? What if they have a copy of "How to Get Whatever You Want from Your Owner by Being Irresistibly Cute" stashed in the closet, and refer to it whenever they need to be especially adorable? Or, in the case of more aggressive dogs, "How to Be the Boss in Your Owner's Home." What if they get together in support groups to learn how to amuse us, or to deal with all types of owners?

What else could be the explanation for some of the things dogs do? What else could explain a dog who follows you wherever you go (even to the bathroom), turns around in circles before napping, jumps on (or even mounts) your visitors, loves the husband but hates the wife or "defends" certain members of the family?

Or are you coping with a dog who steals socks and underwear from the hamper, has a fit whenever a cat shows up on television, insists on wak-ing you up every morning with a slobbery kiss, hates the postman, gives you a ball and walks away, or tries to lick food off your lips?

Or maybe your precious pooch sniffs crotches, rolls in manure, cries when you insist he stay in the other room, picks fights with other dogs, rolls over to request a belly rub or simply acts like a wimp?

Some of that behaviour may seem odd to you, and may make you wonder if there's something wrong with your dog, or with you and the way you've raised the dog. Let's face it – when people finally have to go to an obedience trainer and be told they have done terrible things to the dog's psyche they can be made to feel as guilty as erring parents.

But chances are that even though all this sounds like eccentric behaviour, it's not – at least not its purest form – and you and your dog are OK – or at least will be after you realize the key to living with a dog: your dog is a dog – not a human.

ONE OF THE FAMILY

He may be stretched out at your feet when you're parked in front of the television and practically wave goodbye to you when you leave for work in the morning. He's always there to slobber on you when you arrive home. He's johnny-on-the-spot when you're making a sandwich or the doorbell rings. And he's under your feet when you're doing the laundry, taking out the rubbish and cooking dinner.

He gets his own gift to unwrap at Christmas and his own slice of cake at birthday gatherings.

He sympathizes when you cry or feel sad. He greets you with unmatched passion when you return from a short shopping trip.

You can't imagine life without him, and sometimes you even forget (c'mon, admit it) that he's not one of the kids or a live-in cousin.

But the reality is that inside his head – beyond that body fed by human hands with human-manufactured food and that glistening coat groomed with human-crafted tools and human-created hair care products – he is a product of a long line of dog genes and instincts.

RIGHT *Sometimes you wonder if your dog will ever be OK. But with careful training and understanding, most dogs will learn to behave acceptably.*

LEFT *Sometimes we wonder if dogs get together and have a meeting to share ways to amuse and astound us. Here are three that have chosen a resort setting for their Christmas meeting. Actually, they're only being obedient and obeying the leader of their pack.*

With few exceptions, he comes into your family prepared to act like a dog. You cannot make him act like a human. If you want him to do what you want, to be happy and be among people who are happy with him, you must treat him like a dog. And, in effect, you too must act like a dog, giving him signals he understands.

That thought may make you a little uncomfortable. You're probably picturing yourself walking through a doggie door or chewing on a bone.

ABOVE *This dog's ability to unwrap a birthday gift doesn't relate to anything in the wild and is a learned domestic behaviour. The dog's owners, its fellow pack members, have taught it that good things can be found in such packages.*

But once you understand dog behaviour, you'll realize that it only means you have to make the dog think you're acting like a dog. Once you do, both you and your dog will be OK.

CHAPTER ONE

The Leader
of the Pack

Napoleon, a five-year-old canine, has made his family very unhappy. He runs off whenever he can. He pulls on his leash like Superman proving he's more powerful than a steam locomotive. He refuses to come when called. He growls when anyone touches his toys. He takes food from the table. He barks and growls at everyone. And he has taken over one of the children's beds.

His family are frustrated and are considering having him put to sleep. They say he hasn't learned that he's not the boss – but is he?

Four-year-old Red is very nervous. If he approaches, it's with his head down. Sometimes he has to be coaxed to eat. He hides when the doorbell rings. If anyone raises a voice or a hand, he cringes and rolls over with his feet up.

His family think he's a wimp. They wanted a dog that could act as a watchdog, but this dog is so afraid of everything.

What Napoleon's family don't know is that he sees no reason why he shouldn't be the boss. When he came into the family as a young pup, he wasn't. But he gradually did what any pup would

RIGHT *Submissive behaviour, a product of pack life, is displayed here by the dog rolling over and exposing its underside. The degree to which a dog is submissive is determined by its rank in the pack.*

LEFT *A pack is a group of animals that live together, each dependent on the others for survival. Puppies are born with the pack instinct.*

do – tried to take over and become the dominant member of the family. And they let him.

What Red's family don't know is that he is also reacting to the way they treated him. He may have been a little less aggressive than Napoleon as a pup, but even so, his family obviously never let him get away with anything. His response was to be totally submissive.

Dominance and submission are fundamental components of life for pack animals. Wolves are the quintessential pack animals. And dogs – from the minuscule chihuahua, the smallest dog at 6 inches (15 cm) tall, to the great dane, the largest at 32 inches (81 cm) – are descended from wolves.

THE WOLF PACK

A pack is a group of animals that live together, each dependent on the others for survival. In the wild, the pack supplies protection, companionship, mates, babysitters for the young and hunting companions. Members are loyal and very attached to each other.

Each pack has one leader, usually the most dominant male. He calls all the shots, and everybody else ranks beneath him and must submit to him. Below him, each wolf must be either leader or follower within the rest of the pack.

The leader is often the only male to mate, probably with the "leader" of the female subpack. Because the leader and his mate are the strongest, they will produce strong, healthy offspring. And because no one else is breeding, there won't be too many little mouths to feed. This structure keeps the population manageable, ensuring survival of the fittest.

When male and female leaders have pups, the female becomes the leader of the entire pack until her pups are old enough to travel and hunt with the pack. The sire becomes head wolf again.

Hunting is the reason wolves and dogs are pack animals. They are not fast enough to outrun some prey, so they have joined up in order that they can circle the prey and then attack, leaving no open space for the prey to run to.

Early forebears: Darwin's view

Darwin, the founder of modern evolutionary theory, believed the dog was descended from a mixture of several species of wild Canidae. While this theory is now considered unlikely, there is still something of a mystery about the ancestry of the domestic dog.

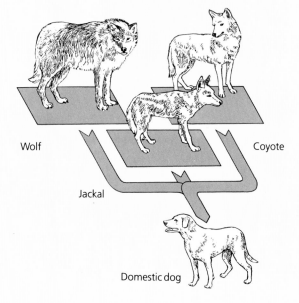

Wolf

Coyote

Jackal

Domestic dog

Once the kill is accomplished, the leader gets to eat first. All the wolves gather around the kill, and if the prey is small, some of the lower-ranking members of the pack may have to wait until higher-ranking members are satisfied and move away from the food.

Because the pack takes care of those who cannot take care of themselves, older wolves are given food if unable to get their own. The lead wolf takes food to his mate while she is raising the pups in the den. Pups are fed by the mother as well as by other adults in the group. They also lick food from the adults' lips, and sometimes the adults regurgitate for the youngsters to eat.

Sometimes the wolves will bury portions of the kill, but usually their stash is found by other animals and the wolves don't reap the benefits.

After the kill and feeding, the pack rests a while, and may spend some time playing. If there is more food in the area, the pack may stay and make the area a home base. The leader will determine when and if the pack moves on. If some members have been separated from the pack during hunting or play, the wolves will howl to gather the pack together.

The leader will retain his position until he is unseated by a stronger, more intelligent wolf or until he dies. There will probably be some fighting among the higher-ranking males to determine who will be the new leader.

A lone wolf cannot survive long without his animal pack. But a dog, even though a pack animal, can survive because he joins a pack of another species – humans.

ABOVE *Even this early on in their lives, puppies understand the need to see who is higher-ranking in the litter. Sometimes this behaviour produces a runt, who is the most needy.*

RIGHT *Dogs like to spend every minute they can with the other members of the pack. When you eat, they eat; when you sleep, they sleep too.*

LEFT *When a dog comes into your home, he leaves his natural pack and becomes a part of your "pack". If you have children, he will probably accept them as younger members of the pack.*

RIGHT *Pushing their way in to get the most and best of everything they can is natural for dogs, and most other animals too.*

BELOW *Dogs will try to make themselves very comfortable on their owners' beds, because in the wild pack animals generally sleep in close proximity to all other members of the pack.*

THE HUMAN PACK

When a dog comes into your family, you take care of all his needs. You provide him with food and shelter, protect him from harm, make sure he is healthy, play with him, and maybe provide him with a mate and help take care of the resulting young.

If he's lucky, you will decide (to a point) what he does and when he does it, and you will be considered top dog. He will receive affection from you, and he will be loving and loyal in return, and it will be a healthy relationship.

When you take a dog into your home, you assume you will be in charge. But if you don't communicate that fact to the dog, in language he understands, he will think he can be leader. You must use consistent discipline to train your dog, but never resort to harsh physical punishment. That would achieve just the opposite, for lead wolves never injure their followers.

If your dog takes over, growls at your every attempt to direct him and even bites you, it

KEEPING A PET

Do Check that everyone in your home really wants a dog.

Do Be prepared to travel some distance. It is usually only breeders of toy varieties that can be found in big cities.

Do Ask to see the dam of the litter. This will give you an idea of what your pup will look like when full grown.

Do Make sure that the Certificate of Pedigree is in order and that this, and the Form of Transfer, have been signed by the breeder.

Don't Buy a dog if you are out at work all day.

Don't Choose a long-coated breed if you haven't time to groom it.

Don't Buy an Afghan Hound when you really set out to buy a Yorkshire Terrier.

Don't Buy a "pet" quality dog if you plan to exhibit it in pure-bred classes.

ABOVE *Modern dogs expend a lot of energy playing, while their wild ancestors expended their energy hunting down prey for survival.*

won't necessarily be because he's vicious or doesn't love you. It will be because he is a pack animal with pack instincts. But if leadership falls to him instead of you, you've got a dog problem.

If you don't take your place as top dog, he won't necessarily be unhappy, at least directly. But you will be unhappy, which will in turn make life harder for him.

If you take command, his instinct to follow will kick in, and you will have his complete attention while you train him to be a member of your household.

It's not uncomfortable for a dog to be ranked below the leader. Once he realizes he is No. 2 or No. 3 or lower, he will adapt his behaviour accordingly and be happy in that spot.

We misread cues from several family dogs before we actually became comfortable with this fact. Like most animal lovers, we assumed that we were showing our dog love by allowing him

to do whatever he wanted (within reason). One look into those puppy-dog eyes, and most humans are pretty much mush when it comes to giving in to a best friend. As individuals with rights and freedoms, we tend to pity any creatures that are in a position to be dominated.

But experience has lived up to research, and we have learned that dogs are happier when they know exactly where they stand. If they have come to accept you as the leader, they will welcome the decisions you make for them and the order you bring to their lives. In fact, most of pack life is devoted to reinforcing each animal's particular position in the pack, even if that turns out to be lowly.

CHAPTER TWO

Behaviour rituals

add could be spotted almost every weekday afternoon waiting at the corner where the school bus stopped to unload his child master. It doesn't take a genius to figure out what the dog was doing. And if you know dogs quite well, it doesn't even take a genius to understand how he knows to do it.

Dogs are programmed to be submissive and develop secure positions very early, many before they are 12 weeks old, and they maintain these positions in order to obtain approval, and thus petting. The way they do this is to develop beloved rituals with their owners. Greeting, hunting, feeding and sleeping rituals are the most common. But they can develop other rituals almost without your realizing it.

The most inherent rituals are based on dogs' biological clocks. Once they have developed habits, they can calculate their activities almost to the minute and carry out behaviour rituals. As long as their routine is preserved, their social position is guaranteed.

Ladd knows that the school bus arrives at a certain time, as the sun moves a certain way in the sky, maybe even after he picks up other noises, vibrations or smells that we can't. And he probably knows that after his buddy disembarks, they walk home, play, and soon after, dinner is served.

LEFT *While howling is for gathering the pack together in the wild, in civilization it may just be a ritual that your dog has come to enjoy as part of his life with you.*

OPPOSITE *Grooming done on a regular basis can become a ritual that the dog looks forward to in his need for order.*

Our dog Timber, a four-year-old cocker spaniel, also knows the school bus that stops at our corner. He uses it to know that some of the neighbourhood kids will be walking by.

Soon after, one of his owners will pull into the driveway, and then dinner will be on the table. Timber has been observed waiting by the door when the appointed time draws near. When his owner arrives, Timber rises and begins wagging his tail and whining even before his other owner can hear the car in the driveway.

The same goes for bedtime. Before our marriage one of us was a certified morning person and the other a night-owl. It took three years to arrive at a compromise of bed at 11 p.m. on

REGULAR ROUTINES

☐ Do try and establish a regular timetable for your dog's walks; for example, early morning and afternoon, and perhaps a short stroll at bedtime. Remember that once the routine is set, your dog will be disappointed if, at the appointed hour, its walk does not materialize, just as it would be if, at dinner time, its dish were not to appear.

☐ The dog whose owner took it for an afternoon walk when it was a puppy will remember and wait eagerly to go out – sometimes long after its insensitive owner has forsaken the habit.

LEFT *This cock-a-poo has come to expect exercise several times a day. If he doesn't get it, he will not only be less fit, he may also feel a little out of sorts because he has come to expect the outings as ritual.*

RIGHT *While this dog is rolling in the grass, probably in something that smells wonderful to him, he is also displaying submissive posture, a ritual that maintains his submissive position in the pack.*

weekdays and an extension at weekends. But with four or five early nights each week, Timber finds it very difficult to deal with the after-11 bedtime at weekends. (Funny, though, how it's OK for him to sleep in later at weekends.)

When 11 p.m. comes and goes, and no-one has taken Timber out for the last time, turned off the television, brushed and flossed or said the word "bedtime", Timber sits in front of the night-owl and whines. Even if the morning person turns in alone, the dog is unnerved that the ritual is not going as expected.

Conclusion? Suffice to say that the night-owl doesn't enjoy staying up late any more because it's not worth the hassle from the dog.

Once in bed, there is that ritual turn before a dog feels ready to lie down – and the way he scratches at the sleeping surface. It has been suggested this is a carryover from when dogs needed to fluff up the grass to prepare a soft spot.

There is, however, a perfectly good explanation for dogs' apparent ritual desire to sleep in their owners' bedrooms. Obviously they want the security of the presence of other members of their packs. But they also want to be there because that's the room that smells of socks and underwear and personal odours that make the dog feel very much a part of its pack. That's also why some dogs have gift rituals. A greeting with a worn sock can reinforce their status in the pack.

DOG RITUALS

Greetings toward humans resemble those toward other dogs. But in dog-dog and dog-human greetings, as opposed to human-human greetings, ranking order plays a role. Allow your dog to socialize with other dogs so he is exposed to these ancient rituals.

When dogs first meet, they touch noses to determine if they like each other. Then they sniff the anal areas. If they like each other, they wag their tails. If they don't, they exhibit "display behaviour", bragging, showing off, pretending to be bigger, showing teeth and growling – all of which can make an opponent feel insecure and anxious to retreat.

When it is over, the dog that has exaggerated most is the winner. This often resolves the question of which is the stronger and therefore should rank higher without resorting to actual fighting. However, a fight will ensue if there is any doubt.

A fight begins with the dogs facing each other, with stiff tails, growling through raised lips. If the hair on the neck, the back and the tail is raised, a fight is imminent. This battle usually looks and sounds worse than it is. Growling and snarling are used to alarm the rival, and usually the louder the noise, the less real danger.

Fortunately, as soon as one of the dogs realizes it is weaker than the other, it lies on its back and exposes its throat. This submissive gesture is a sign of surrender, and the victor backs off.

Once submission has been determined, the submissive dog will greet the other after even a brief separation with the "wolf greeting" – excitedly nipping, licking and smelling the mouth of the dominant wolf.

When you say "good dog" to your resident canine, you are adding psychological reward to the greeting ritual as well, which explains why it seems to send your dog into ecstasy.

CHAPTER THREE

How does my dog love me?

You've had a really hard day. You overslept and got stuck behind a slow wide load on the way to work. Someone was parked in your space, and you had to walk three blocks in the rain without an umbrella.

You lost a filling at lunch, which resulted in an emergency trip to the dentist. You still have a million things to do when you walk in the door. And instead of giving you an understanding hug, your spouse picks a fight with you.

You just can't take any more, so you retreat to your bedroom, feeling as if you don't have a friend in the world, and have a good cry.

That's when Leia appears at your side. She gently reaches out to you with a paw, lays her head on your shoulder, pushes her nose into your face and emits a sympathetic whimper. You're so grateful that you have Leia, who loves you so

much that she feels what you feel and wants you to feel better. You have such a wonderful dog.

Well, you probably do have a wonderful dog – but not necessarily because she "loves" you. She may be very attached to you and be very dependent on you. But what she feels for you cannot necessarily be called "love".

But, but . . . what about Lassie? Certainly she loves Timmy. Doesn't Toto love Dorothy? What about Millie and Barbara Bush? Tramp and "My Three Sons"? Astro and George Jetson? Dino and Fred Flintstone? Benji and everybody?

What are all those classic dog stories about if dogs don't love? If Leia doesn't love you, how could she be so adoring, so devoted, so loyal? Unfortunately, she isn't really adoring, devoted or loyal. The love you see in her eyes is all made up in your mind.

BELOW *Because dogs follow the leader of the pack, your dog will want to be where you are, involved in what you are doing, even if he doesn't understand the purpose of your action.*

MOOD MONITORS

☐ One of the reasons why dogs bring great comfort to humans is their uncanny facility of picking up our moods. The dog, in common with its ancestor the wolf, is sensitive to atmosphere. That is why it will come and sit quietly beside us when we are despondent or jump around enthusiastically when we are in high spirits.

☐ Dogs have an inbuilt sense of time. How else would they know to draw attention to themselves when a regular feeding time draws near?

☐ It has also been proved that dogs can recognize places, even if they have not visited them for months, or perhaps years. In fact, a dog that has been sleeping quietly in the back of a car may get up and show considerable excitement within a half-mile or so of a once familiar location.

LEFT *A dog who appears to be showing you how much he loves you is extending the "wolf greeting", which consists of nipping, licking and smelling the mouth of the more dominant wolf.*

OPPOSITE *Dogs that seem to sympathize are not showing love as much as they are picking up on your moods and attempting to make you act again in the way that makes them feel secure in the pack.*

When Leia exhibits the traits you interpret as love, she is behaving like a pack animal. Dogs do not think or act logically in human terms. It is wrong to expect human actions or reactions from them, and you and the dog will be better off if you learn to treat her as a dog and let her live in harmony with her innate needs.

Because you are the leader, any change in your moods affects your dog. In a wild pack, if the leader snarls and pushes a member of the pack out of the way, the lower-ranking animal will take on a submissive posture and move aside. If the leader cuddles up to another animal and engages in a little relaxed play, there's no reason not to join in and feel that everything's OK.

So if you come home smiling and bubbling, the dog will be elated. If you're miffed at your boss, the dog might be a little more anxious. She

would prefer that conditions are always normal. When things aren't, she comes to you in a questioning manner. She wants to be reassured that your out-of-the-ordinary mood is temporary. If you're unhappy, she's unhappy.

This self-concerned behaviour became evident in our house after the first few times we raised our voices to Timber during training. A dog who learns his lessons sometimes too well, he took this one a step further. He knew that a raised voice meant he was in the wrong. But that lesson made him sensitive to any raised voice, even when it isn't directed at him.

We discovered this during a husband-wife argument, when Timber took on a submissive posture and pushed his way on to the wife's lap for reassurance and comfort. (This doesn't mean your dog will always go to the woman in your

HOW DOES MY DOG LOVE ME? **25**

family for reassurance. The choice of the wife was probably for two reasons. First, in our family, the husband early on took on the role of leader, and the wife filled in as security blanket. Second, the wife's raised voice, although anxiety-producing, is still less threatening than the husband's.)

Loving owners that we are, we stopped arguing and reassured Timber the pack was stable. We have no statistics, but we agree that there have been fewer, or at least shorter, arguments in our family since we discovered Timber's sensitivity.

Just because your dog doesn't exactly love you doesn't mean you can't love her and let her know it. Be sure you don't have any great expectations. Many of us mistakenly treat our pets as children, and because of their dependent nature they end up fulfilling that role. Some people, especially those without children or those who may be recovering from the loss of someone close, have a tendency to use the dog as a substitute child or loved one. You will be sorely disappointed if you expect your dog to give as much as she gets, or if

RIGHT *Many dogs act jealous by trying to push their way into the family circle when hugs or kisses are exchanged. This is because of their natural desire to maintain their rank in the pack.*

LEFT *Bonding is a necessary first step in effectively training your dog. When she is secure and confident, she will be happy to approach and learn from you, her leader.*

you subconsciously believe she will always be there, even though you know she probably cannot live more than 10 or 15 years.

Whatever you call it, the two of you can still have a very satisfying relationship. Over time, and with special attempts, you can form a close emotional tie with your dog through bonding.

BONDING

In animal terms, bonding is the pairing of two creatures who develop a long-term connection as the result of shared experiences. It gives animals the desire to stay with each other, to be secure with the other. It is stimulated by face, voice and eye signals, and cooperative behaviour.

Bonding is very pleasant, but it is also a necessary first step in training your dog. When she is secure in the pack, she can be confident in your dealings with her. When she is aware of her place in your life, she feels happy. That can make you happy. And it is much easier for a happy owner to train a happy dog than an unhappy owner to train a dog who is unhappy, fearful and doubtful

MOOD MONITORS

❑ When you bring the dog into your your house, do not crowd or scare her. Gently allow her to look around, and when she seems somewhat at home, bring in members of the family individually and let them handle and talk to the puppy.

❑ Just like a human baby, she won't yet understand what you are saying. But she will be comforted by the tone of your voice. You can change her mood as quickly as you can change your tone. A harsh utterance can snap her out of a playful jaunt, a friendly command can assure that she comes, and some baby talk can elate her.

❑ A lot of bonding involves touch. Your dog will eventually look forward to the way you stroke her fur, pat her head and allow her to fall asleep in your armpit as you stretch out on the couch. Whatever you do as long as it does not hurt the dog, will help you become intimate.

of her status. If she bonds with you, she will be very eager to please you.

Usually you have no idea what your puppy experienced before you got her. She may have socialized with other dogs and humans, she may have had little contact with others, or no good contact at all with humans. In any case, you need to communicate with her that she is safe with and accepted by you before you even think about rigorous training. It won't hurt to begin gentle housetraining, but it's best if you take time to get to know your dog and allow her to explore.

For a while, you won't get much tenderness in return. Like a toddler who doesn't want to be held – there are just too many toys to play with –

she'll squirm away if there's any energy circulating in her frisky body. Then one day, you'll find a lump forming in your throat when your pup actually approaches you for physical contact. A head on your lap, a chin on your ankle, an expectant look into your eyes, a paw on your chest – these are all signs of successful bonding.

If these bonding sessions are welcome, your dog could come to expect them as part of his routine. Our dog Timber, for example, delights in snuggling and then playing with his ball as an after-work bonding ritual.

Bonding also involves introducing the dog to the family's routines. Show her there is a time to play, exercise, eat and sleep. Allow her to keep you company as you perform your chores, and take her with you on errands or outings in the motor car if you can.

Playing is especially important for bonding. Get down to her level on the floor. Allow her to "attack" you, roll around, cuddle, run away and make a noise if she wants. Allow her to misbehave during play so she can gain some confidence.

In the animal world, bonding can occur between mates, parent and offspring, or just two middle dogs in the pack. It's best if every member of the family bonds with the dog, and it's OK if everyone's bond is different. The dog will accept whatever relationship arises as long as she knows what to expect. The person who takes the dog for walks, feeds her and accompanies her to the veterinarian may have a different relationship with her than one who merely plays with the dog on occasion, but nevertheless satisfying for both.

At our house, the dog is bonded well enough with the wife that he "pouts" when he sees her getting ready for work. However, since she's

LEFT *Getting down on a dog's level is a way of making the dog comfortable because he doesn't automatically feel submission due to your largesse. Children have an advantage in this area because their faces are already less threatening.*

RIGHT *Because your dog is attached to a member of his pack (your family), he may also become attached to things that remind him of the pack through smell or shared experience.*

gone every day, he's over it soon after she leaves. The husband, however, works at home, so the dog depends on his being there most of the time. When he packs a suitcase and leaves the house overnight, the dog spends the evening lying at the front door.

DOGS AND CHILDREN

Most dogs are naturally well disposed toward children and will form a special bond with them. They smell great (to a dog), drop food (eliminates the begging step), have lots of toys (and sometimes they take the dog's), are always active (watch for quick turns) and are short enough to be easy

marks for licking. They also bring out a dog's natural instincts to protect the younger members of the pack.

Of course, not all dogs love all that acitivity. Some breeds are especially good with kids, and others are unenthusiastic or even antagonistic toward them. Dogs who may not have been socialized well can be unpredictable around children. Even a normal dog who has had a bad experience will learn to distrust them. That's why it's important to teach children how to handle a dog.

It's best if the child waits for the dog to come to him or her. Do not make any abrupt move-

LEFT *Dogs are especially attracted to children because they smell great, drop food often, are very active, are easily kissed and have toys to play with.*

ABOVE *Children should never pull a dog's ears, tail, fur or anything else on the dog. Instead, because a dog may react with a display of dominance, they should be taught to wait for the dog to approach them and then touch it gently.*

ments. Let the dog sniff the back of the child's hand, and if she seems to be friendly, pet her gently.

Never allow a child to pull the dog's ears, tail, fur or anything else that might seem pullable.

Even a good-natured dog can react to pain. Give the dog plenty of time for sleep and quiet time. Children can also assist with caring for the dog as a way of bonding.

DOGS AND BABIES

Dogs are especially attracted to babies because they are even more interesting, better smelling and need more protection than older children. The dog's first reaction will be to sniff the baby, which will be OK for both, but be careful about letting her lick because it might scare the baby. Some people also worry about transmission of

germs through a dog's mouth, but this isn't a concern if the dog is clean, vaccinated against germs and free of parasites.

Dogs can become jealous of just about any member of the family, but there is more chance of this in relation to a baby because usually family members are overly concerned about the baby's welfare and tend to notice the dog less.

All dogs will play what are called jealousy games because they react in accordance to pack social rules of dominance and submission behaviour. Dogs that butt in on displays of affection simply feel threatened. They see others getting attention and recognition and join in for fear of being left out. Their natural desire to maintain their rank is what makes them seem so jealous.

The most difficult form of jealousy can occur in families in which the dog came before the first child and is considered by the parents to be practically a first child herself. In this case, introduce the dog to the smells of the baby before the baby enters the picture: diapers, powder, special food, nursery. Also, try not to alter the dog's routine.

The dog will feel that she is in more control if the baby is sleeping the first time they are introduced. Once she gets used to the sight and smell of the baby, then she is in more of a position to handle the sounds and the movements. Reinforce good behaviour.

Don't neglect the dog in favour of the baby or isolate the baby from the dog. If the dog sees that the baby is kept separate from the pack, she might get the idea that the baby is not part of the pack and try to drive him or her away by growling and nipping. If the dog is only ignored or reprimanded when the baby is around, she will feel separated from the pack, blame it on the baby, and try to work her way back into the pack, which could lead to behaviour problems.

No matter what, remember that babies and young children should *never* be left alone with a dog. No matter how much you trust the dog, or the child, there is always the possibility of either overreacting to something the other has done and attempting to inflict pain. What started out as a happy relationship can turn ugly very quickly when you have to decide who did what to whom and whether the dog is stable enough to stay in the family. The dogs are usually the losers, which is unfortunate because the real blame usually should be placed on the parents who failed to follow this rule of dog-kid relationships.

LEFT *Baby Nicole can get away with just about anything with this great dane, but it's still not a good idea to leave them alone together just in case the dog decides to enforce dominance.*

RIGHT *If you treat your first dog like a child, decreased attention to him in favour of a new baby is likely to make him insecure about his position in the family pack.*

RIGHT *The person who takes care of the dog in your house might have a much closer relationship with the dog than someone who just plays with her once in a while.*

LEFT *Fighting between pet dogs may occur when the established dominance relationship changes through illness, or the younger dog grows assertive. There may be a power struggle with fighting over food. The owner must handle the situation carefully.*

DOGS AND OTHER PETS

Another thing that might bring out jealousy in your dog is the way you treat her in relation to other dogs or pets in the household. Your dog will probably assume that she is No. 1 under all the humans in the family, so any other pets should rank below her. Although you probably want to treat all your dogs alike, the dogs need you to choose one to be higher in rank. Always greet, feed and care for that dog first. That reinforces her dominance and lets all the dogs know where they stand. It sounds like the kind of favouritism that humans are always complaining about, but it's what the dogs need.

The owner may be unaware of the established pack order between pet dogs, favouring the underdog — the smaller, older or weaker.

Dog in a Manger

This will upset the natural order, causing the dominant dog to defend its position by attacking the favourite.

The owner should show affection to the dominant dog. The position of both dogs will be defined, the hierarchy accepted.

CHAPTER FOUR

Understanding your dog

Our cocker spaniel, Timber, was four months old when we decorated the house for Christmas that year. The Christmas tree went up on a platform next to the window, stockings were hung from the doorway, lights adorned the windows and a strip of silver sleigh bells was hung from the doorknob.

Timber was just about housetrained. He was taken out at regular intervals and seemed to understand the concept. But sometimes he needed to go out between the scheduled outings, and he had not yet figured out how to let us know when.

Some dogs bark or whine, but those things never occurred to him. He knew what to do when we told him to "speak" (especially for food), but he was either too timid or too polite (or too stupid, we sometimes thought) to relate it to asking to go out, even when we suggested it.

Instead, he handled it by getting as close as possible to the port of exit and looking around for someone to lead him outside. Sometimes we'd have that eerie feeling you get when someone's staring at you and we'd look up to see him sitting by the door fixated on one or both of us.

Then one evening we were startled to hear the sleigh bells ring and both ran to see who had dared to open our door without knocking. But the culprit was only Timber, sitting by the door, after having given the sleigh bells a poke. And just for good measure, with his full audience now present, he poked them with his nose again.

BELOW *This dog is telling you that while she is perfectly happy to lie here on the bed with this very comfortable stuffed dog, she is also interested in what the other members of the pack are doing and will change plans if you want.*

Whether he really meant the ring as a signal to go out is still in question, so we're not really bragging about our dog. The point is that we "rewarded" him for the deed by taking him out. So the next time he needed to go out, he rang the bells as a signal to go out.

Ever since then, not just at Christmas, those bells have hung from our front door for Timber to ring when he needs to go out. (In fact, he has a second set on the door at the house of a relative we visit frequently.)

He's four years old now, so he doesn't need as many unscheduled outings as he used to. Three or four times a day is fine for a grown dog. But once in a while, when we've forgotten or lost track of time, we hear the bell ringing.

Not every dog is lucky enough to have bells. All most dogs have is a lot of moving body parts and a few vocalizations, ranging from whimpers to growls to barks and howling. If you listen to your dog, you will gradually learn what each sound and motion means.

VOCALIZATION

Arf, ruff, woof, yip – no matter how you spell it, a bark generally means the dog doesn't know what's going on and is stalling until he can decide (or have a decision made for him) what to do.

If the dog is submissive, a continuous bark when someone approaches the house is directed to the owners. His job, as a lower-ranking member, is to alert you. Reassuring him that you are

RIGHT *Tundra obviously has something to say about the pattern of this quilt her owner is making, in the form of a howl. She probably receives positive feedback for this howling and continues to do it because it seems to please the leader of her pack.*

LEFT *Barking in this case means "I'm stuck in this fence and I'd really like some help getting out" and should be taken very seriously. While many dog owners hear just one or two types of barking, dogs have a wide variety of barks for different communications.*

handling the situation is more effective than any-thing else to quiet him. A dog who considers himself leader will be more apt to continue bark-ing since it's his territory he's guarding, not yours.

It's usually necessary to note the context of the bark. If the dog barks during a "wrestling" ses-sion on the floor, he's probably just excited. If he barks in the car when a vehicle pulls up alongside, he's probably feeling that his personal territory is being invaded. If he barks at birds and other dogs on TV, he's probably somewhere in between those two situations.

Some breeds bark more than others, and some individual dogs bark more than others. Some-times it depends on the environment in which the dog is raised. A dog living with a retired person might be less prone to noise than one in a family with kids who rough-house a lot. A dog who is teased might bark more than one who is treated with respect and love.

If your dog barks after you give him a command, he is defying you. It may seem cute,

but if you let it go uncorrected, it could be just one step toward his self-election as leader.

No matter how dangerous a barking dog sounds, the adage usually applies that you don't have to worry so much when dogs are barking loudly; they are more threatening when they are quiet or growling.

Growling is more aggressive than barking and should be taken as a warning to stop what you are doing or to keep your present distance. It may be accompanied by a raised upper lip, a crinkled snout and bared teeth, which is prime posture for biting. A lot of growling could be a sign your dog considers himself top dog and feels the need to protect what he thinks he has. Some-times this happens when the dog has not received constant training and is then suddenly corrected. Alternatively, he may be responding to constant abuse.

Dogs learn that whimpering or whining can get them what they want. The first time we noticed Timber using this tactic, he was sitting

outside the bathroom door looking desperate and whimpering slightly.

Assuming he wanted to get into the bathroom, we opened the door for him. But he only went in and stood by the toilet, whining even louder. When asked what he wanted, he poked his nose at the toilet set and whimpered again. On a hunch, we checked his water bowl; and sure enough, it was empty. When we filled it he took a long drink and went on with his life.

We can't prove that's what he intended, but we now take whimpering seriously at our house. Any time one of his toys gets thrown under furniture or carried into an inaccessible corner by one of our ferrets, Timber whines and points his nose toward it.

Howling is something we usually associate with wolves, but dogs howl, too. In wolf packs the

LEFT *In the wild, a howl is an expression of unity, a way of gathering the pack, a meaning this Siberian huskie has translated as "Let's get together to race on this sled dog team."*

ABOVE *Poking his nose into a water source may indicate the dog needs a drink and his water bowl is empty or inaccessible.*

howl is an expression of unity – a way of communicating over long distances, to gather the pack, maintain territory or get in the mood for hunting. Your dog may not have the full moon or a ridge in the wilderness to make his howl as eerily romantic as those in literature or films, but if he feels separated from the family, he may embark on a howling session. This separation feeling could come from being left alone in the house too often or simply being locked in another room.

Facial Expressions

Menacing facial expression of the dominant dog.

Submissive pose of a dog which accepts its owner as pack leader.

RIGHT *Facial expressions are an important method of communication for dogs, with ears, eyes and mouth conveying a range of feelings. Bright eyes and a protruding head contribute to the quizzical expression on the face of this dog.*

Howling is so instinctive that dogs tend to join in whenever they hear another dog howling. All the dogs in a former neighbourhood of ours used to get involved in a howling session whenever any of the dogs felt the need. And many house dogs can't resist when they hear a howler on TV.

BODY LANGUAGE

Dogs' next best thing to vocal communication is what they can do with their tails. Sometimes there's so much emotion in the tail that it seems as if it starts at the waist. A wagging tail is said to mean indecision, but if accompanied by a happy face, it probably means the dog is full of joy.

Allowing for differences in conformation according to breed, if the tail is extended horizontally, it indicates contentment; if sticking up, excitement or alertness; if lower between the legs, fear or tension.

Facial expressions are not as easy to interpret. Some owners say they can see when their dogs are "smiling", but people who are not around the dog as much usually think those owners are just one step away from "seeing" UFOs and little green aliens in their back yards. But from two dog owners to others: if you think your dog is smiling, he probably is.

"Smiling", however, has to be taken in context. Your dog probably won't be smiling when being corrected or just after arising. But he might be after chasing a rabbit, in the midst of play or when you get visitors.

Even if he's not smiling, if his ears are poised, his eyebrows raised, his eyes glistening and his movements bouncy, he's probably a pretty pleased pup. If he's just caught his ball from across the room or been praised for obeying a command, he's probably overjoyed.

If his ears are flat and his lip is raised, he may be fearful or uncertain. If his ears are flat and the lips show lots of teeth, he's preparing to attack. If his ears point forward and his muzzle is open, he's ready to attack.

As you can see, ears are crucial to determining expressions. But don't forget to take into account what type of ears your dog has. Ears can range from the pointed ears of the German shepherd to the lop ears of the dachshund. Words such as "raised" or "flat" can mean very different things among breeds.

Unfortunately, some breeds are at a disadvantage because their ears and/or tails are docked. This practice was developed so the ears and tails of hunting dogs could not be easy targets

for wild animals. Tails were also docked to prevent injuries while the dog was tracking.

Since most cropping is now done because the cropped look has become the breed standard, it might be time to stop. Most dogs are now pets, not trackers and hunters, and docked dogs are hindered in the way they can communicate. If you are waiting for a puppy from a breeder, request that it be totally intact when you pick it up. Otherwise, you may find that cropping has automatically been done.

Another thing dogs have to communicate with is the tongue. Used for lapping up water and food, cleaning and maintaining body temperature,

The dog's expressive body language

The diagram shows the various body postures and facial expressions by which

the dog communicates giving the consecutive changes from the normal stance to submission.

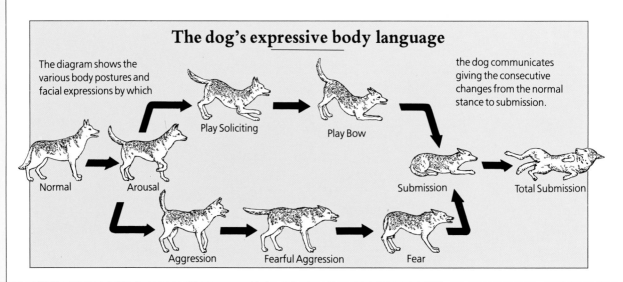

Normal   Arousal

Play Soliciting   Play Bow

Submission   Total Submission

Aggression   Fearful Aggression   Fear

it also plays an important role in expressing affection and gratitude.

You may even have been subjected to a "wolf greeting", when the more submissive member of the group greets a more dominant member by nipping, licking and smelling the latter's mouth. In most dogs, this usually ends up just licking because humans tend to discourage the nipping and don't understand the smelling.

Although some people worry about the germs that can be conveyed through this greeting, it has never been proved that diseases are actually transmitted this way. Probably more harm is done to dogs when they are told they cannot greet in this manner; they react by feeling separation from, and insecurity within, the pack.

We are among the dog owners who have been criticized for "spoiling" our dog and "treating him like a child" by letting him do this and other instinctive actions that meet with disapproval. But we are treating him more like the pack animal he is than do those who deny his true needs.

DOG LANGUAGE

Here are a few other things you might need to know about what your dog is telling you, directly or indirectly:

☐ When your dog lies on his back, his underside totally exposed, he is proving his submission to you.

☐ Dogs have sweat glands all over their bodies, but full cooling occurs only by the movement of air over the dog's wet tongue. That's why water is so important for your dog. If he refuses to answer a command and is panting, he may be telling you he needs a little time off.

☐ A dog sprawled flat on the floor is not necessarily suffering from heat or exhaustion. He may also be showing you he is relaxed and content.

☐ When a dog gives you his paw without prompting, he may be asking for something. This action is instinctive in dogs, as they learned early on that kneading their mother's teats stimulated the flow of milk. As adults, this becomes a begging gesture. This explains why it's so easy for most dogs to learn to "shake".

☐ Jumping on a wolf who comes home with a kill is normal behaviour for pack animals. That's why a dog might jump on you as you enter, especially if he smells groceries or a new toy.

☐ In the wild, only the lead dog makes direct eye contact. Dogs have learned they can make eye contact with humans even if they are submissive. But if yours combines eye contact with growling or some other aggressive behaviour, he may be telling you he's feeling a little dominant.

CHAPTER FIVE

The meaning
of words

There is a gag in use among many cartoonists – we believe we first saw it in a "Far Side" cartoon by Gary Larson – that depicts a man and his dog, Ginger, in conversation.

The man, very agitated, is saying something like "Ginger, I'm really upset with you. That was a perfectly good shoe. But look at what you did to it. It looks like some of your leftover food that's been sitting around for days."

The dog, smiling and content, is actually hearing "GINGER, blah, blah blah-blah blah blah. Blah blah blah blah-blah-blah GOOD blah. Blah blah blah blah blah blah blah-blah blah FOOD."

In other words, Ginger is understanding only three words: "Ginger", her name; "good", which the man usually uses to mean he is pleased with something that Ginger has done; and "food", which Ginger has learned to mean something good to eat. So the message the dog is actually putting together from all this is, "Ginger, good, food" – a message quite different from what the man intended.

RIGHT *Dogs learn to recognize their name and other important words through repitition, and will comprehend their words even in other contexts.*

As exaggerated as this cartoon example may be, none of us who has lived with a dog can deny the reality of it. Dogs may not understand English as a language, but they can learn to understand some words in whatever language their owners speak, and all the junk we put around the key words falls on deaf ears.

We have joked about how much fun it would be to teach dogs the wrong meaning of words – "go", for example, when we mean come, "come" when we mean "sit" or "run" when we mean him to speak – or even nonsense words for all his commands – "plant" for sit, "pudding" for come or "supercalafragilistic" or some such word for roll over.

We didn't actually do that, for the same reason you don't name your dog something like "Edward" – it's not the kind of word you want to be yelling from the back door when you call the dog. Nor do you want your dog to look stupid when you tell it to "fetch" and it rolls over. But the concept does show that dogs learn the meanings you teach them.

We tried just about everything to make our puppy grasp the concept of "Come!" – praise . . . pushing him across the room . . . pulling his leash . . . treats . . . and finally enticing him with Oogie, his favourite tug toy.

Oogie did the trick. He simply couldn't resist "coming" when he saw the latex dog face that he had had the pleasure of sniffing out and unwrapping for Christmas. We used it to reel him in to the "come" command, and rewarded him with a tug session at Oogie's expense.

Sometimes we tried it without Oogie, and he was reluctant, but always agreeable in the end. We had finally trained him to come. Our complacency lasted only a few weeks. One day when asked to come, he took a little side trip to pick up Oogie along the way. Apparently, the dog perceived our reward as our intent, and so when we stopped using Oogie, he felt something was missing and tried to recapture that pleasure.

For months, no matter where the object was, the dog would run to fetch a toy on his way – even after he traded in Oogie for a rubber ball as the toy of choice. ˙

Only after months of training with commands like "no", "now" and "just you" did he learn that "come" doesn't always mean "bring your ball here". Even today, he still slips up and grabs the ball if it's at his feet as we say "Come!"

The moral of the story is be careful what signals you give while training. Your dog does "understand" commands, but not according to the dictionary definition.

Through repetition, your dog will come to associate events, actions or objects with specific sounds and words. This is how a dog learns to recognize his own name and words that mean important things.

If you say "walk" enough times as you take the dog out for one or pick up her leash, she will get to know what it means. Even if you say it in some other context, the dog will think you mean her and whip her head around to show interest.

LEFT *Your dog loves to hear you talk even when you are not giving commands, especially if you say nice things in a kind tone of voice. It makes the animal feel secure in that all appears to be status quo with the pack.*

RIGHT *It's especially important for a dog to be able to understand his owner in a situation like this. Otherwise, the dog might injure himself trying to make his own decisions.*

Your dog loves to hear you talk even when not giving commands, especially if you say nice things in a nice tone of voice. She will especially go for that high-pitched baby talk that many people use with dogs because animals in the wild communicate in a high-pitched tone if they are friendly. She will not like your deeper tone because animals in the wild communicate in lower tones if they are aggressive.

Your tone can say a lot even if she doesn't get a clue about the context. Some dogs react to any raised voice, even one not directed at them, by cowering or seeking comfort. Dogs who hear pleasant conversation will be relaxed.

You will need three voices to communicate with your dog: a firm, gentle voice for commands, a yelling voice for correcting and a baby-talk voice for praise and bonding. Use the correct voice in context since dogs will read these signals as they are given.

SIGNALS AND BODY LANGUAGE

The art of detecting signals from humans is born from the way members of a pack interact, using sounds and body language to express emotions and wishes. Because of this previous "experience", your dog also picks up body language from you, opening the way for training, either intentionally or unintentionally, with hand signals and other cues you might display.

These non-verbal leads are almost a necessity for dogs learning to work in films, on television or in other areas of the entertainment field. Sometimes they have to work at a distance from the trainers, or the trainers have to be "quiet on the set" during filming but still get the dog to do what her part requires.

The dog may also learn to pick up non-verbal cues that we never intended. When we carry ourselves too casually, loosely gripping the leash, a dog with a tendency toward aggressiveness may

try to take control. When you hold the leash securely and walk confidently, the dog gets a more positive message.

Some dogs, however, are intimidated by too much authority in posture and will react by being overly submissive. The average person already towers above a small dog, preventing her from making facial contact, so it's best to stand a foot or so away and get down to her level sometimes.

Your hands should be used only for actions that your dog will associate with positive bonding: petting, scratching, hugging, feeding, playing and training. Never use your hands to hit the dog or hold its muzzle shut or anything else the dog might interpret as aggressive.

If a dog backs off when hands reach out to her, she has probably been abused. Assure her she is in no danger in your household. You want the dog to trust you, but don't expect miracles overnight. It is a long process.

When touching this type of dog, bring your hand up from the ground, palm up, starting with the underside of her chin, or offer your knuckles to her nose for sniffing. Never reach out to her in a manner that makes her think your hand is coming toward her (especially from above) to hit her as it will only frighten her.

Only the lead dog makes direct eye contact in the wild, but dogs have learned they can make eye contact with humans even if they are submissive. Be sure you are not accompanying your glare with unfriendly postures. Most dogs can handle the posture or the eye contact, but put one with the other and add a human growl, and some dogs will be truly frightened. This might sound like fun, but if you do it too often, you could erode the bond you have made with your friend. Some dogs react by being totally submissive and urinating uncontrollably.

On the other hand, if you need to quiet a dog, this might work. But beware that an aggressive dog may be provoked to attack.

We also tell our dogs a lot of things we never mean to by our actions. Throwing off a blanket in the morning can mean getting out of bed. Putting on a coat means someone's going outside. A suitcase by the door means someone's going away overnight.

BELOW You will need three voices that replicate tones that dogs use among themselves to communicate with your dog: firm for commands, loud for corrections and "baby talk" for praise and bonding.

CHAPTER SIX

Your wish
is my command

One summer a relative was planning to look after Timber while we went on vacation. "Will he listen to me?" she asked. "What do I say to him to make him behave?"

To assure that she would be in control (which we knew would also be better for the dog in the long run) and that our best friend would feel secure in his temporary environment, we wrote down a few commands (see box).

The list is not to show you what a wonderful dog we have. It's to show the potential for dogs to learn commands. In all honesty, we planned to stop after the usual few, but after we learned how quickly he picked up words on his own it became fun to see what he was capable of.

Since we raised him like a submissive pack animal, he spends most of his time looking to us for cues and commands. It may seem like a

LEFT *"Release" is the command this hunter uses to ask this German shorthaired pointer to give up the quail it has just delivered. It's also a good command for the surrender of toys and other objects.*

DOG COMMANDS

We have listed more than 60 words that our dog Timber lives by – he actually knows a few more, but we left off people's names and some other personal words – in the hope that they may help you choose commands for your dog.

Word/action *What it means to Timber*

All gone/surrender with hands *Give up asking for food*

Back up/motion away *Back up a step or two*

Bad dog *They hate me; I'm out of the pack*

Ball *Round object (my security blanket)*

Bath *An hour of torture in water*

Bird *Something to watch and chase*

Bed *Large, soft nest in bedroom*

Bedtime *Everybody in the bed to sleep*

Bone *Something to obsess over*

Burger *Food!*

Catch/hold up ball *Snatch in mouth when thrown*

Come/pat chest *Come*

Cross *Cross the street*

Door's open/open the door *Sit by the door and look out*

Down (playing) *Get off furniture*

Down (eating) *Stop begging*

Downstairs *Go down the stairs*

Drink *Receive a drink*

Fetch *Fetch/find something*

Get him up *Kiss whoever is still sleeping*

Get the . . . *Chase and grab something*

Give it to . . . *They give me something in my mouth and tell me to deliver it*

Go ahead *Keep walking*

Good boy *I feel a kiss coming on*

Gooooood booooooy *Boy, am I wonderful!*

Go . . . *Followed by something good, like ride or walk*

Go get the mail *Go directly to the mailbox and sniff around (sometimes I get to carry an envelope or a small box)*

High five/hold up hand *Slap hand with paw (or slap air if too far away)*

Home *The place we come back to*

Hug *Put paws around neck and kiss*

In *Get in car, house or room*

Kennel *Where they send me when they really hate me*

Kiss *Lick 'em till they can't stand it*

Lie down/point to floor *Lie down*

Look what you're doing *Unwrap leash from tree or pole*

Move *Get out of the way or get stepped on*

Nice *Gently take food from hand or fork*

No *Don't do what I'm doing or thinking about doing*

No barking *Stop barking (momentarily)*

Off the bed *Get off the bed*

OK *Do what I'm thinking of doing or resume what I was doing*

On the porch *Get to the porch either from driveway or from inside house*

Other paw *Slap or shake with other paw*

Out *Go out for daily duty including a walk*

Out the back *Go out the back door alone for just a quick duty*

Over there/point *Move in that direction*

Paw/hold hand out to shake *Shake paw*

Pills *Four good (yeast and garlic) and one yucky (heartworm)*

Push (door) *Open a (unlatched) door*

Push (playing) *Push ball down the stairs or off the bed, or wherever it will roll*

Rabbit *Fast creature I chase outside*

Ready? *Bark or grumble to show I'm ready to catch or play*

Release *Give up ball or toy or food or whatever's in my mouth or under my paws*

Ride *Sitting in the car and usually ending up somewhere fun*

Right here *Heel to the left side of leader*

Sit/point over head *Sit*

Speak/hold food or object *Bark once, more if something I really want, like meat or cheese*

Squirrel *Fast creature I chase outside until it runs up tree*

Stay *Don't move*

That's enough *Stop doing something (like kissing or growling)*

Up/hold hand over head *Jump up and snatch something*

Up on the bed *Get on the bed*

Up on the couch *Get on the couch*

Upstairs *Go up the stairs*

Wait (food) *Sit with restraint while food is put down for me (followed by "OK")*

Wait (outside) *Stop at kerb before getting OK to cross*

Walk *Go for a long outing, with lots of time to sniff, mark territory and chase intruders*

Wanna . . .? *Usually followed by something good (like "Wanna go for a walk?" or "Wanna fetch?")*

shallow existence to humans, who have hopes and dreams and egos, but nothing makes the dog happier than pleasing you. If you let him, he will spend his entire life (except when he's exhausted) making sure he is doing what you want.

He's comfortable in this position because of his heritage as a pack animal. In the wild, wolves cater to the wishes of the leader: they eat when he eats, hunt when he hunts, sleep when he sleeps, get out of his way when he wants them to and play when he initiates it.

Dog owners are sometimes criticized for this type of behaviour in their dogs. "You might as well be confining him in a cage for his whole life", the critics say. But if they really knew dogs, they'd know they're arguing for their own needs, not the dog's. Of course, you have to know how to train your dog to attain this kind of relationship. It doesn't just happen.

TRAINING

Training can begin at approximately seven weeks. First the dog has to get used to his collar and leash. Try the collar first without the leash, and then a few days later attach the leash and let him drag it around for a period each day.

Only one family member, preferably the dog's leader, should train the dog at first. Be aware of your tone of voice, your hand signals and posture, your dog's personality and your dog's mood.

Experts recommend three tones of voice for dealing with a dog: a firm voice, used normally and for commands; a yelling voice, for correcting, and a baby-talk voice, for praise and bonding. Most dogs respond attentively to the normal voice, with submission to the yelling voice and elation to the baby-talk voice.

Training denies your dog every impulse that is natural for him, so it may take him a while to

hear your commands and understand your goal. It can take up to three sessions for a dog to respond to a new command.

If you use hand signals correctly, your dog will learn a separate hand signal for every command. Eventually the hand signals can be used alone, so choose hand signals you can live with.

If the dog is affectionate, you'll be able to use affection as a reward. If he is more aggressive, be firmer. However, no matter what his temperament, the time to train him is not when he is tired. You can tell by noticing what else is happening in the room, too. If there are children or other pets, or someone is putting on a coat to go out, your dog will be distracted.

Unless your dog is in advanced training for obedience trials or showing, sessions should be limited to 15 minutes. He will enjoy learning new commands and tricks, but because repetition over a period is the key, there's only so much he can learn in one day, anyway. His attention span is such that he bores easily unless he gets a break. Because training tends to tax a dog so much, he will probably want to nap soon after each session.

THE COMMANDS

Name The first thing you should teach your dog is his name. He won't ever really understand the concept of a name as such, but he will know that when you say that word you want his attention. If you use his name when you talk to him, he will learn it. When he responds, praise him.

Sit To teach "sit", hold the dog on his leash so he must hold his head up. Then, as you say the word, push his rump down. After a time, just moving your hand over his head and saying the word should do it. If your dog needs more incentive, hold a treat instead of the leash over his head.

BELOW *At the end of a training session, always remember to pat the dog and give words of praise.*

RIGHT *Apply pressure to the dog's hindquarters to encourage it to respond to the command "sit".*

FAR RIGHT *When teaching a dog to sit and to follow any other commands it is important to select a quiet* *locality because any distractions will upset the dog's concentration.*

The Command "Sit"

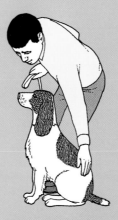

With the dog standing still, give the command "sit". Gentle pressure over the hindquarters as shown may first be necessary to evoke the required response.

Sitting is a natural posture for dogs and they should feel quite happy in this position.

You should be able to kneel down, keeping the leash held high, without upsetting your dog.

Lie down We have found that dogs have a really tough time understanding the concept of "lie down" from a standing start. You'll find it easier if he is seated. Then push down on his neck until he lies down. If you have to, pull his front legs forward. If he tries to get up, repeat the command and push down on his back.

Stay "Stay" is a command that can save the dog's life, above and beyond being obedient. It can assure that he sits at the kerb as traffic goes by, for example.

Once the dog has learned "lie down" or "sit", "stay" is the next step. Tell the sitting or lying dog to "stay" and then move away a little. If he gets up, push him down and repeat "stay". Increase the distance each day. When he stays even when you are out of sight, he deserves more reward. If he has a tough time with this one, use his leash, and as the person in front moves away, the person behind him holds him back.

Come If your dog is going to be outside without a leash, "come" is crucial. Teach it inside and

The Command "Lie down"

The command "down" is especially important for large dogs, so that they do not cause problems in the home. From the sitting position the dog's front legs will need to be lowered, as shown here.

LEFT *Training is a sequence of lessons, and at this stage you can move back towards the dog and slip off its leash. Always leave the collar on under these circumstances so that you can restrain the dog more easily, if it attempts to run off.*

OPPOSITE *Once the dog is sitting, you can then extend the leash on the ground. Hand signals are an important part of the trainer's repertoire, the raised hand here indicating "stay."*

OPPOSITE BELOW *We have often joked about how much fun it would be to "confuse" dogs by teaching them the wrong meaning of words: "go" for example when we mean "come." Dogs learn what you expect when you say the word, not the actual meaning of the word.*

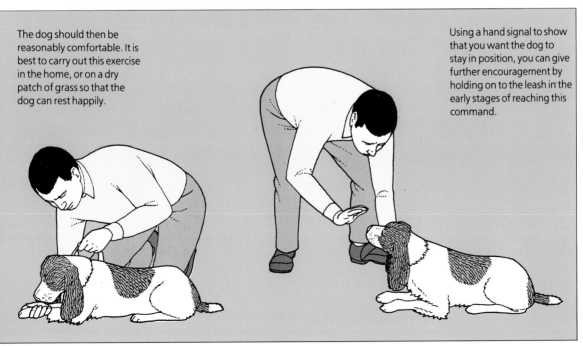

The dog should then be reasonably comfortable. It is best to carry out this exercise in the home, or on a dry patch of grass so that the dog can rest happily.

Using a hand signal to show that you want the dog to stay in position, you can give further encouragement by holding on to the leash in the early stages of reaching this command.

RIGHT *Lhamar, a 12-week-old lhasa apso puppy, is learning to get used to his collar. Once he does, he can move on to command training.*

BELOW *If you use hand signals in conjunction with voice commands, your dog may eventually learn to follow the hand signals without ever hearing the command.*

then move outside. This works best with two people. One holds the dog from behind and the other goes across the room and tells the dog to come. The dog will be thrilled if you get down on his level and will be more inclined to come to someone he can actually reach. If bonding has been pleasant, he may come without incentives. If he needs motivation, hold a treat or, using the leash, pull him over when you give the command and praise him when he arrives. Start not more than a few feet from the pup, and gradually increase the distance.

Once he has grasped this concept inside, try it outside, but definitely use the leash out there to ensure he doesn't run off and get into trouble.

Never call your puppy to come when you plan to punish him. He will associate coming to you with being punished and will see this as a reason not to come to you.

No Use "no" whenever you want your dog to stop doing something. Say it at the crucial time. After the dog has jumped off the couch is no time to give him a "no" for being on the furniture. "No" at that point applies to getting off the furniture. If you've said "no" at the right time before,

he knows you don't want him *on* the couch; now you tell him you don't want him getting *off* the couch. At this point he's more confused than anything – see why timing is so important?

If you watch your dog carefully when he's close to doing something wrong, you're likely to catch him before he acts, which is the appropriate time for "no". Wait until he has obeyed the command, and then praise him for doing so. His mother did something similar when she showed him what actions she disapproved of by making a noise or a motion to deter him.

When issuing positive commands it helps to use the dog's name followed by the command. However, if you use "no" with the dog's name he may come to associate his name with a negative. So be careful.

Release When you say "release" or "let go" to a puppy, he should let you take away whatever he is playing with. At first he will growl and defend his possession, which is how he behaved with his litter mates when he had to assert himself for whatever he could get. Even though it's a natural reaction he needs to be deterred, or he will refuse to surrender some object that may harm him or some expensive sweater you bought for a special occasion. It's much easier to teach this to a puppy with baby teeth than an adult with larger teeth.

Practise this with his toys and food, so he doesn't have to learn in a state of emergency. Be sure to praise the dog for giving up what he is guarding so closely. After a while he will come to think of it as a natural response because it pleases you, his leader.

LEFT *"Stay" is probably the command these dogs were given to make them wait on the back of this truck until their owner comes out of the store.*

OK Use "OK" when you want him to know he is released from whatever discipline you previously expected of him. When Timber is told to "wait" while we set food down for him, "OK" is what releases him to eat the food. When he has "come", but he gives you that look that says he wants to be somewhere else, "OK" lets him know when he can leave.

"OK" can also be used to show that everything is all right – after he is attacked by another dog, for example, or if he's feeling sensitive to arguing voices. Don't say "OK" though if everything really isn't, or he'll learn not to trust your word.

Heel Even if your dog is always on a leash, heeling is important. If he doesn't heel then, he'll be dragging you along by the leash.

Let the puppy get used to the collar and leash before you ever venture outside. First let him drag the leash around for limited periods for a few days and then start holding it and walking with him. Talk to him when you do this so he will connect the leash with you being pleasant and see it as a point of contact with you.

The next step is to take him outside. Once he is accustomed to this, start teaching him the "heel" command, keeping the leash short so he has to stay by your side and pulling back on him if he tries to get ahead of you.

We use the term "right here" for Timber because it works in the house, too, when we need him at a certain spot. The actual word you use is not as important as letting your dog know what you mean. If possible, give your dog a chance sometimes to run off excess energy without the leash. It will be almost as much fun for you as it is for him as you watch him bouncing around tracking squirrels and rabbits.

Collars and leads for different activities

A suitable collar should be selected for the dog, with several leads for different activities. Pictured below are:

1 long leather lead
2 nylon slip lead
3 check chain
4 heavy rope handline slip for kennel use
5 town lead for tall dogs
6 long training rope
7 strong plaited leather lead
8 hand-sewn, rolled leather collar
9 puppy collar with elasticized inset

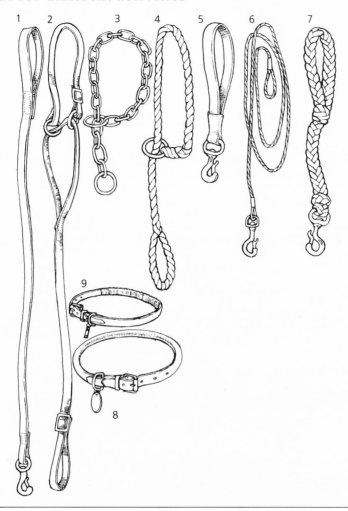

The leash

Be careful putting on the lead, so as not to frighten the pup.

The dog may be playful or nervous during the first lessons.

Hold the lead in the right hand, reassure or admonish with the left.

The lead should be slack with the pup walking at the owner's pace.

TRICKS

"Does he know any tricks?" is a question other people tend to ask about your dog. Tricks are those things your dog does on command that aren't for manners or safety reasons. You probably don't want your dog to know as many tricks as a circus animal or a dog who "acts" in the movies, but it can be fun to learn some things beyond the basics. As long as there is no abuse involved in the tricks you teach your dog, he will enjoy learning at this advanced level because it keeps him occupied, allows him to spend more time with you and pleases you.

The following tricks are not those your dog needs to know for a dog show. Nor are the commands above given according to show standards. If you want to train your dog for showing, check with the appropriate breeding organization for standards. However, if you just want to enjoy your dog, here are a few primary tricks to try.

BELOW *A dog who really enjoys "fetch", as well as swimming, can be trained to combine the two passions.*

RIGHT *Jo-Jo's owner, obviously an equestrian, has trained the dog to ride this rolling horse toy.*

Speak First make him sit, then hold up food slightly over his head and tell him to speak. You may need also to use "wait" or "stay" to keep him from jumping up. If he doesn't understand, bark once yourself. After a while he might try to combine sit and speak when he sees the food.

Shake Put your hand out while saying "shake", and if necessary, put his paw on your hand. Food rewards help this one along.

Roll over Not the easiest thing to teach a dog who likes to keep his feet on the ground.

Command him to lie down then, using food, trace a circle in the air to the side you want him to roll to, helping him along with a gentle push, first on to his back, then over on to his other side, and finally into the lying position again.

BELOW *Tricks like "up" are easy to train when the dog is given food as a reward. Dogs see food as a reward because their acceptance in the wild pack means they get to share in the food of the pack.*

RIGHT *When your dog exhibits the traits you interpret as love, she is merely behaving like the pack animal she is.*

PRAISE

While the dog is mastering his commands, you have to master praise. As you show your dog what you want, praise him so he knows what he can expect. The first time he performs correctly, reinforce his behaviour with a special treat (but work out these treat calories in relation to the dog's daily intake). Once the dog has mastered the lessons, the treats can be phased out. Eventually, praise will be enough.

Praise can make some dogs feel that they can return to what they want to be doing, so give just enough to let him know you are pleased with what he has done – don't overdo it.

CHAPTER SEVEN

Bad dog,
get in your bed

ike most puppies, ours went through a period of being a "bad dog". If he wasn't tearing tissues, he was chewing socks or – worst of all – not doing his duty outside and then messing on the bed while we were brushing our teeth. We don't even like to think about how many times we had to strip the bed and blow-dry the mattress before we could settle in for the night.

We repeatedly told him he was a bad dog and showed him the mess, saying "No" (note: we didn't rub his nose in it). But we might as well have been talking to a wall, it seemed.

Knowing how much he enjoyed pack activity, we finally decided the thing that would have the most impact on him would be exclusion.

We briefly called him a "bad dog", then cleaned up the mess while he watched from afar. We didn't say another word – for almost 45 minutes. Every time he came near, we ignored him. By the time Timber finally crawled over and began to lick our toes, we were starting to miss him as much as he missed us.

We then adapted that method to the more common tactic of confining him to his kennel crate as punishment. The next few times he messed, we scolded him with a "bad dog", then ordered him to "go to your kennel" and placed him in the crate.

One day soon after, we found a mess on the bed, but the dog wasn't near it. We found him cowering in his kennel, ears down, eyes questioning, body posture extremely submissive.

Whenever we found evidence of "bad dog" behaviour after that, Timber was nearly always cowering in his kennel. Soon those incidents decreased and eventually ceased altogether. We still have a kennel, but we can't remember the last time we found the dog there or had to send him there.

Sometimes, when our dog gets a little lax, and there is danger he may be retraining himself because we haven't been on the ball, we ask him "Do you want to go to your kennel?" and he then obeys the command. All he needs to hear is

RIGHT *A dog that repeatedly fails to respond to commands, may have to be sent to his bed for some separation time to make him realize that you do not approve of his behaviour. Dogs in the wild would similarly be separated from the pack for unacceptable behaviour.*

the word kennel, but it helps that we put it in the form of a question, because he then knows it isn't a direct command.

The sight of that dog in the kennel the first time was certainly worth a good laugh. But the incident was even more valuable in that it was a real turning point in the dog's development. He had finally learned that when he acts in certain ways, we are not pleased with him; and when we are not pleased with him, we separate him from the pack. And that's the last thing a dog needs.

Although this incident shows how dogs learn to avoid what you consider to be unacceptable behaviour, unlike humans, they don't think in terms of right or wrong. They don't feel remorse

about chewing up your sweater or messing your carpet. What they feel is your reaction. They will try to stop doing what you don't like simply because you don't like it. If you weren't so upset with them, they would see no reason to change their behaviour. If you praised them for uncontrolled chewing, they'd try to do more of it.

This relationship between owner and dog is not so different from the one a wolf mother has with her young. She disciplines by grabbing the puppy by the scruff of its neck, holding on to as much skin as possible and shaking the pup without lifting it off the ground. Humans can add a "no" to this movement, which makes even more of an impression on the puppy.

ABOVE *If this setter had been more attentive to commands given by his owner, he might not have ended up with a snoutful of porcupine quills. The dog needs to relearn his submissive position in the pack.*

LEFT *It's natural for dogs to chase moving objects because they try to outrun prey as pack animals in the wild. Even so, the practice can be very harmful to the dog and should not be encouraged.*

RIGHT *Chewing by puppies is usually caused by teething and can be curbed by supplying ice to numb the animal's gum pain and designating only certain safe toys to bite. Older dogs in the wild pack would allow such chewing during this period.*

No matter what it is that keeps your dog in the dog-house at your house, do not make a big deal out of the incident, scream at the dog or hit him with your hand or a rolled-up newspaper. All that does is make the dog afraid of you. Think of what you do as a "correction", not a punishment, and the goal of correction is not to make you feel better, but to let your dog know that you do not accept that particular behaviour. You will get results with patience, repetition of training, praise and rewards.

Dogs need discipline when they are young. As pack animals they will try to rise as high in the pack as they can by playing dominance "games". They will run away, pull on their leashes, bite, bark, growl, nip, chase, steal and chew. Here's how to deal with some of the most troublesome behaviour from your dog.

HOUSETRAINING

You can certainly use the method above if your dog is almost housetrained, but ideally, house-training is a process that begins when you bring your puppy home.

ABOVE *Running away with your hairbrush may be a sign that your dog needs attention or wants something of yours so he can feel close to you when you're not there.*

Until that time, your puppy probably lived with litter mates in a pen where they relieved themselves at any time and in any place they wanted to. So the puppy may have a difficult

---

THE BASICS

☐ If you are out at work all day, it is unfair to keep a dog no matter how much you may love them, unless, of course, you have a friend or helper who could be relied upon to call at your home every noontime to exercise the pet in your absence.

☐ Never, ever, hit a dog. Your tone of voice should be sufficient to express displeasure and a dog wants only to please. Be generous with praise whenever a dog does well, patting it, and saying, "Good boy", or "Good girl", as the case may be.

Housetraining

1 When your pup relieves itself, place it promptly on the sheets of newspaper that you will have placed on the kitchen floor.

2 Soon the pup will look for the newspaper when it needs to answer the call of nature and will toddle on to it, but be prepared for the occasional mistake.

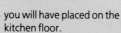

3 Gradually decrease the amount of newspaper and leave a sheet or two by the back door.

4 Soon, if the weather is warm, you can open the back door when the pup heads towards it, and encourage it to go outside.

time understanding that there are rules on the matter in her new home.

One place the puppy didn't want to relieve herself before she came to your house was in the sleeping and feeding area of the pen. This is called the "denning instinct". If you keep the puppy in the crate when you cannot watch her, and remove her and take her outdoors to relieve herself at regular intervals, she will probably wait because she'll think of the crate area as her den.

The crate should be of a size appropriate to the dog. Let her have a toy so she has something to do; the idea is not to punish her but to make the environment feel like her den. Do not leave food in the area, though, or you will have trouble keeping track of when she needs to go out.

With a young puppy, there will have to be at least six trips a day. If you wait too long, she might have no choice but to go in the den. Be sure to take her out after she eats, drinks and wakes up. Try and establish a routine early on.

When you can watch over her, let her get her bearings outside the crate. If she looks as if she's ready to make a mess, grab her and rush her outside. Clues might include wandering around restlessly, pawing an area of the floor or turning in a circle.

Some experts say that if you're too late to catch the dog in the act, it's no use reprimanding her. But dogs know their own scent and need to be taught what they cannot do as well as what they should do. Lead the dog to the mess, make sure she sees it, and tell her "No" as you smack the floor near the mess.

The mess should then be cleaned immediately, using a cleanser that removes the odour as well as the mark. For territorial reasons, dogs like to reuse the same spot. If she can't find that spot through the odour, she may hold off until you can get her to her favourite spot outside.

After a few weeks, your dog should have fewer accidents and need fewer trips outside as well. Nevertheless, you may have to keep to this routine for six or seven months until the pooch is fully housetrained.

If your dog is shy, don't correct her for wetting in the same manner you would an outgoing dog; she needs more love and affection than discipline.

Some apparent housetraining problems are in fact other problems, even though the manifesta-

LEFT *Puppies will often relieve themselves more readily on an area of short grass, rather than bare concrete. In order to prevent damage to a lawn, they can be trained to use one restricted area.*

RIGHT *Stealing a child's toy can be a sign that the dog is jealous of the attention the child gets.*

tion is the same. For example, a dog who is ill or on medication may have an accident and be as mortified as you would be if you suddenly wet the bed one night.

A dog who loses a few drops of urine during greetings or when someone rings the doorbell may be reacting overly submissively. This may be especially true if he also raises a paw, lifts a hind leg, rolls over or exposes his underside. Overly intimidated dogs may also develop behaviour problems like wetting, chewing, barking, or biting.

BARKING

If you have established yourself as the leader your dog will probably limit his barking jags, but dogs who see themselves as leader will bark whenever they feel the need. Some dogs bark to get what they want or if they feel threatened, and others just get carried away by stimuli too good to pass up (such as other dogs on television or a family wrestling session).

The key to cutting down on barking is for you, not the dog, to get control of his habit.

Don't yell or throw water at him. Instead, note what makes him bark and ask him to bark.

Reward him with a food treat for this barking when he does it on command. Practise when he isn't already barking, asking him to speak to go out, for a toy, for whatever he wants. He will soon focus his barking in your direction, giving you control over it and him an outlet for barking.

Once you have gained this kind of control, you can start telling him to stop barking sometimes. Since you want him to bark in a real

How to stop your dog barking

Although a dog may be wanted because it will bark at intruders, a dog that barks persistently is a nuisance.

Dogs must be taught at an early age to stop barking when ordered to.

Gently raising one's knee to a large dog's chest is a good way to prevent it from jumping up.

A roll-up newspaper banged on the table will catch the dog off-guard, and should stop it barking. A vocal command should accompany your actions; for instance, "NO."

Water squirted over the dog from a hose may be effective. This measure is also sometimes adopted to stop dogfights.

RIGHT *Shoes, socks, underwear, blankets, furniture and toys can be among the victims when your dog decides that anything is fair game for a chewing attack.*

emergency you don't want to communicate to him that he can never bark, so use "enough" instead of "no".

If he barks when you are away from the house, trick him into thinking you have left the house (go far enough away so he can't smell you) and, when he barks, surprise him with "enough".

CHEWING

Furniture, blankets, shoes, socks, other clothing – just about any object that strikes your puppy's fancy can end up in her mouth. Confined pooches have even been known to chew on doors, baseboards and walls. A previous dog of ours actually swallowed washcloths from the laundry pile whole and survived their trip through her digestive system.

In a puppy the problem is usually that she is teething. You might try giving her several ice cubes in a bowl. The coldness will numb her gums and relieve the pain. Also let her know that some objects are chewable and others are not. Don't give her too many toys or you will be perpetuating her understanding that anything is fair game for chewing. Try to limit her to three items. When you find her with something you don't want her to chew, correct her and replace it with a chewable.

In older dogs the problem is not hunger; more often they are anxious about being alone and chew to relieve their emotions. They become bored or frightened that you will not return.

You may need to change the dog's lifestyle so she is no longer bored and has no energy to burn off in chewing. Occupy her mind with games when you are there.

If your dog's chewing problem just won't go away, try a spray or solution from the pet shop to deter chewers.

STEALING

If part of your cheeseburger slides out from between the bun and your dog snatches it from the air on the way down, she is not stealing.

TEACHING YOUR DOGS TO SPEAK

Just as it is possible to teach a dog to "speak" with a bark when it is shown a treat, then by lifting a warning finger to encourage it to speak "softer, softer" until the mere whisper allows it the prize, so it is possible to prevent a dog from yapping persistently in everyday life.

After all, most of the time, what falls, or is thrown onto the floor is hers.

But if she sneaks upstairs while you are busy and pulls underwear out of the hamper, she is a thief. Dogs also steal socks, pillows, stuffed animals, and gloves, hats or toys from the kids they love. Some can't resist tissues or worse, out of the bathroom waste bin. Some unspayed females steal and shred paper and such before going into heat. There is a reason behind these acts.

Most of the time the dog does not destroy what she steals. Even if it starts out that way during teething, later she usually ends up just cuddling with it, as a baby would.

Some owners, unfortunately, think that this, like chewing, is done out of spite. But dogs are not capable of spite, and what appears to be spite is actually motivated by anxiety. You can't tell him when or if you'll be back, so he frets about being left behind. The dog knows nothing of your life and all your obligations besides him. All he knows is that he needs and wants you.

If what he takes is a favourite object, like a child's doll, he may be trying to steal the special attention the child gets. He may be using it as a substitute for members of the pack who don't have time for him. Or maybe it's something you used as the object of play, so he has special feeling for it because he shared it with you. You need to make him feel more secure in the pack with the use of physical contact, discipline and a clear pecking order.

GUARDING

Even more neurotic than stealing is guarding an object. If he carries object love this far, try to get rid of the particular object. Often this is a dog who has not had limits set for him – his owner may have been too harsh one day and too lenient the next.

Let him know that you expect him to obey commands each and every time they are given, not just when and to the extent he wants. "Come" does not mean he can look at you and just sit

there. "Come" means what it says, and not just approach you, but come to exactly where you have let him know your standard is, usually by pointing or gesturing.

A friend of ours taught his dog he meant business by using a different tactic. "I only tell a dog to come once," he said. If the dog didn't respond, he'd lead her by the collar or, if necessary, pick her up and carry her to the appointed spot.

No matter what approach you use, be sure to praise the dog when he does respond to your

intensive retraining. Then he will learn that good things come with his good response.

Some dogs are prone to object attachment only when they feel they are being threatened. A dog that lives with a childless couple, for example, may feel uncomfortable and territorial when relatives' children enter his home and play with his toys, because he is not used to sharing.

We knew that this was a possibility with our dog, so from the start, whenever he walked by with a toy "growing out of his mouth", we made

LEFT *A dog who guards an object, such as a bone, from his owners may need to be shown what his limits are.*

RIGHT *A dog has to know that he must obey commands under any circumstances – even when it puts him in a position that makes him feel vulnerable.*

RIGHT *Keeping your dog out of your flower beds is possible if your dog has come to respect you as the leader of the pack and has been shown his limits.*

a point of asking him to surrender it on command. "Release", he was told, whenever he resembled Linus of the Peanuts cartoon, who constantly holds a security blanket.

At first he suffered through this reluctantly, sometimes even growling instead of surrendering. But every time he gave up a toy, he was rewarded with praise and usually a play period with said toy which was good compensation.

That may be the reason we seem to have toys constantly dropped on us by this expectant hound. But a few minutes of play a few times a day seems a small price to pay for not having to constantly worry about a dog attacking a child for innocently showing interest in a bright object that bounces.

TRESPASSING ON FURNITURE

If you don't want your dog on certain pieces of furniture, it's best not to allow her on any furniture. That includes your bed because your dog can't distinguish between shapes of furniture; all she knows is that it's all soft and off the ground. However, you might be successful in allowing your dog to use your furniture, but not allowing her to get on furniture in someone else's house. If she has learned "no" and "OK", this can work quite well.

If she ventures on to your furniture only when you are out or in another room, you need to play a little trick to deter her. Some experts recommend several mousetraps or aluminium foil under a blanket or other covering on the couch. The dog will be quite startled when she jumps up and creates a noise.

SUBMISSION GAMES

Although dogs must be trained to be submissive to their owners, they should not be overly submissive. That results in problems such as shyness, self-inflicted wounds, excessive salivation, involuntary urination, car sickness, fear and too much attention to the private parts. Such dogs can also become overly dependent on the owner, turning into grovelling, pathetic wimps. Although some owners love it (chances are they even encourage it), the dogs are domineering in their own way by playing on the owner's emotions.

To help prevent this kind of attachment response, be careful how you correct the dog. Say "no" only once, and don't get too emotional about it. The dog should not be made to feel you are angry at her or ready to engage in battle. She should only know that you don't want her to perform that action again.

CHAPTER EIGHT

How intelligent is my dog?

As a youngster, one of us had a chihuahua, Tiny, who used to do dog stuff in the field behind the house. One day she was seen romping with a group of children not from the neighbourhood, and later on that day she was nowhere to be found.

Nobody will ever know for sure whether she was stolen or was having so much fun with the kids that she followed them when they moved on. Fortunately, two days later, she returned to the house with sore, bloody feet, the result of walking probably miles to get from wherever she was, anxious to get home.

Tiny wasn't alone in being able to find her way back home. Scores of books and films have told stories of dogs who wanted nothing more than to return to their masters. But the trick isn't

magic; some say dogs have a homing influence related to the magnetic north pole; others say it's their ability to use their senses to be always aware of what is occuring in their environment.

The odour of certain flowers near your porch, the particular sound of your car engine, the sight of your front steps and possibly other sensual cues that we can't even begin to understand all combine in your dog's mind to let him know which house is yours. If he has returned home it is probably because he followed the scent tracks he made on the way out.

Another important element in your dog's triumphant return is his desire to come home. He has an instinctive need to be part of a pack and if you have made him understand that you are the leader of the pack, he will do everything he can

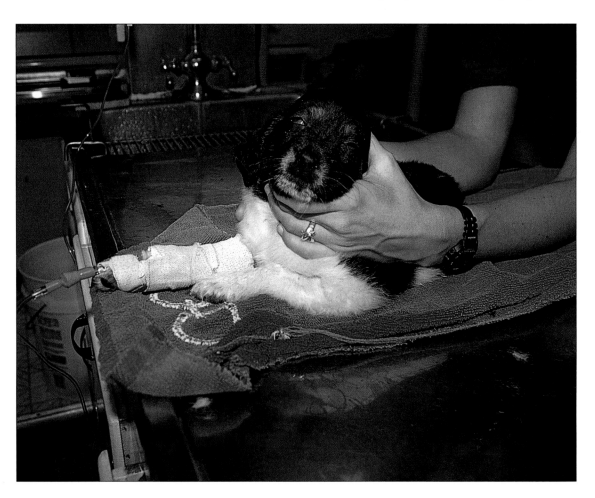

to try to return to you. However, if he sees himself as a leader, he's just as likely to stay out there somewhere and find a new pack to follow him.

RECOGNIZING PLACES

We first noticed Timber's ability to orientate himself on a trip to visit a relative an hour away, a journey we make with the dog approximately once a month. As soon as we pulled into the appointed town, the dog began whining excitedly, obviously in anticipation of our destination 2 miles (3 km) on the other side of town. He had whined like this in the past as we pulled into the driveway, but he had never started this far away from the house before.

The next time we went there, we tried a different route. But, as if he could read the borough limit sign, Timber began his whining almost at the edge of town. We have tried two other routes since then, and even made sure we don't give him any signals – yet he always whines a certain distance from the house.

Maybe it's something in or about the house that he can smell from afar. Maybe it's the odour of some industry or animal or tree species in the town. Maybe it's the sound of the water plant. Maybe it's because the car slows down and stops at junctions after a continuous journey on the highway. Or maybe he can sense when 55 minutes are up and expects he'll be there in another five.

RIGHT *Most dogs are intelligent enough to master complicated tricks like this Hollywood dog learning to carry a bucket "stolen" from a "villain."*

LEFT *A trip to the veterinarian can be unpleasant for an injured dog. He may remember what the place looks, sounds and smells like, and will be frightened there in the future.*

ABOVE *The smell of these wildflowers, as well as the surrounding images, may be helpful in showing this dog the way home if he wanders too far and gets lost.*

RIGHT *The people who abandoned this stray dog along the side of this desolate road might be surprised to find that he can navigate his way back to their house, using sights and scents that humans may not even notice.*

THE PAVLOVIAN DOG

Above The Nobel prize-winning scientist Pavlov pictured watching an experiment of the type which led to his famous theories of animal behaviour.

A dog's training can progress from simple toilet training through the basic commands such as "heel", "sit", "wait", "come", "down" and "stay", to the complex training of dogs who compete in championship obedience classes. The essential principles used in training are similar whatever is being taught, and it is these which owners should try to understand. By the application of these principles, any dog can be taught at least the basic commands, and most much more than that.

Some breeds tend to be more responsive to advanced training than others, and it is noticeable that the majority of dogs who compete in obedience championships are border collies. When dogs fail to learn even basic training this is almost always due to the training, or lack of it, rather than the dog. Nevertheless, there is a tiny minority of dogs with genuine mental or behavioural problems due to their genetic background or severe distress early in life.

The process of training a dog is essentially that of conditioning him to perform a particular action from his normal repertoire at a specific moment. In order to train a dog successfully, it is helpful to understand how conditioning works in the dog's mind.

Two kinds of conditioning are recognized by scientists. Classical conditioning was discovered by the Russian scientist Pavlov early this century while he was working with dogs. In his now famous experiments, Pavlov found that his dogs always salivated when they smelt their food on its way. Their meal time was always signalled with a bell. Pavlov then found that after a time, his dogs would salivate in response to the bell alone, even if no food was offered. It can be seen that this type of conditioning works through a process of association in the dog's mind.

RIGHT *This travelling dog may be able to remember this street once he leaves and is obviously intelligent enough to stand under the shelter on the back of the truck during the rain.*

This also works in reverse. He knows when we are a block from home and begins the same I-know-where-we-are antics. Whatever the exact reason for this, it gives us first-hand proof that dogs do have memory. How well they use it may be an indication of their intelligence.

CANINE INTELLIGENCE

Intelligence in dogs and other animals is a much-disputed issue, especially when different breeds are considered. Expert trainers measure intelligence by how fast a dog learns new tasks. But even then, individual temperaments and degree of successful socialization as a pack animal can make a difference.

Certainly most dogs understand some signals and are fairly obedient. Most are also capable of linking two ideas, thanks to their innate need for rituals. That's how it was so easy for Pavlov's famous dogs to associate the sound of a ringing bell with feeding time.

But their association is very literal, so they find it more difficult to associate events separated by time. That's why it does more harm than good to punish your dog for something he did an hour ago. You can't treat him like a child who has to "Wait until your father/mother gets home". If

the other "parent" walks in the door and corrects the dog, he'll learn that just sitting there annoys that person and he will avoid the person as much as possible. As a dog owner, your goal is to make the dog associate you with good things. Positive reinforcements, such as a pet or some baby talk every time he walks by, can make the dog want to return to you without threats.

IT SEEMS LIKE PLAY

☐ Work should be interpreted by a dog as play.
☐ When a Royal Air Force sniffer dog is being trained, his reward is to retrieve. When a young dog retrieves a package of cannabis he will be allowed to have a game with the package, but that will be the only game he is allowed when working.
☐ A dog's instincts are channeled into retrieving a particular scent. The dog gets every individual scent and breaks it down in its head until it finds the one that it knows its master desires, regardless of what else is with it. The dog builds up a "scent picture." Every picture given to the dog includes the drug or explosive that the dog has been trained to find as a common denominator.

CHAPTER NINE
People who dislike dogs

There are people who don't want to sit on furniture where a dog has been, cringe at the thought of a dog licking their cheek and jump back a few feet when a dog breezes by. They will most likely be the ones the dog will offer a slimy toy to, beg from at dinner, choose to jump on when it gets excited about company or even, at worst, mount.

Such people make dogs out to be the most dangerous, foul-smelling, unappetizing predators on the face of the earth. If their attitude is that negative, it's probably the result of one or a series of unpleasant experiences – or at least lack of experience with well-trained dogs.

Nevertheless, if you've got one of these people in your family, chances are nobody is going to ask that person to make allowances for your dog.

How dare you put your mere canine above a blood relative? No matter how unjustified the attitude, you'll have to make doggone sure your dog doesn't offend anybody.

LEARNING THE RULES

Jumping Almost any dog will jump on people if he is excited, happy and untrained. If the dog is not supposed to do it, then that rule must apply to every situation. You cannot let him jump on you in play and then ask him not to when you're wearing a silk dress. This will only confuse the dog, which leads him to jump on anyone who pays attention to him. To teach him not to jump, say "no" when he does and praise him when he stops. He will soon understand that he doesn't have to jump on you to get love and praise.

LEFT *Jumping on a wolf who comes home is normal behaviour for pack animals. That's why a dog might jump on you as a greeting.*

RIGHT *A person afraid of dogs might be wary of approaching this hardware store in view of the dog on guard at the door. But if the dog has been taught that his rank in the pack is lower than all humans, he should not pose a problem.*

Aggression A little defiant growl when we issue a command never fails to give us a chuckle, but if it starts to become habitual we start taking it seriously. Talking back, and growling while eating, when he is corrected or when you put his leash on him is a sign of a dog who is aggressive.

Each incident may seem isolated and harmless, but it's all one problem – the dog thinks he's in charge so he resents it whenever you try to act as if you are. You may also be giving him mixed signals. If you call him over and pet him to calm him down when he growls at someone, he thinks

he has been praised for growling. Instead, he should be corrected at the critical moment.

To retrain, you may need to make use of a leash, using it to jerk the dog back when he displays aggressive behaviour. If you have a truly aggressive dog, limit his time rough-housing so he doesn't see it as the norm. You might also need to send him "to his kennel" when he gets out of hand.

Total retraining can start with his learning to accept your brushing him. If he won't allow it, send him to his kennel. Reward him for any success in this area, and gradually increase grooming time. Side benefits of this exercise are less shedding and a prettier dog.

Snapping Teething causes puppies to snap or nip to ease the painful pressure of incoming teeth. If you allow them to, they will be happy to bite your hands, fingers, arms and toes. Even though you know you are only playing, the pup will not understand that it can bite your hand but not that of the neighbour's child. If the habit has already developed, let him know its days are numbered by use of "no".

Sniffing and mounting It wouldn't take long for your standing in the community to fall if you went around greeting people by sniffing their crotches, but in dog society sniffing is expected. Somehow it gives them an idea who has the higher rank in the pack.

LEFT *Some children are afraid of dogs and should not be pushed into being with them unless the introduction can be made gradually. If the dog is too dominant, he may be aggressive towards the fearful child.*

RIGHT *If someone in your household is wary of dog hair, he or she may not approve of your dog making himself at home on the furniture. The dog will probably assume he can go where the other members of the pack go.*

Another "obscene" habit dogs exhibit is mounting. The dog, usually an unneutered male, places his paws around some part of the human body (usually a leg) or a piece of furniture and carries out the motions of sexual intercourse.

The problem may begin around the time the puppy reaches sexual maturity, which is also a good time to have it neutered or spayed to prevent this and, more importantly, any more unwanted pups in the world. In an older dog, mounting may be the result of frustration over never mating. Dogs with more aggressive, dominant temperaments may also be more prone to mounting.

If you are not going to neuter the dog, make sure he gets daily exercise, keep a check on him near women you know are menstruating (family member or close friend) and see that he doesn't get too attached to anybody.

If he manages to mount, try to correct him with a "no", before he gets too far along or he may snap at you. You may have to physically remove or restrain the dog or make a loud distracting noise. Don't worry if your dog seems

interested in humans of the same sex he is. Given the social environments that we expect dogs to become a part of, a little bisexual nature is normal.

Running away Many owners take their dog's running away as a sign that the dog does not like the family. The real problem, again, is that the owner has not got through to the dog that the latter is not the leader of the pack.

Take every measure possible to make sure the dog does not run away, including establishing dominance, keeping him on a leash, or fencing if necessary.

If and when your dog runs away, do not chase him. If he sees you following, he will continue to lead. Instead, stand your ground. If necessary, start walking in the opposite direction. He will then become concerned, even startled, that you

ABOVE *Dogs who go "over the wall" may not have accepted their owners as leaders of the pack.*

are not following and probably return. If he continues running away, follow him in a vehicle or on foot, perhaps with some kind of bait (food/treat).

When he returns, be sure to reward him with praise. If you scold him upon his return, he will associate your scolding with his return, not with his departure.

CHAPTER TEN

Hunting instincts

Wolf puppies are born with an instinct toward killing, but they do not have an inbred knowledge of how to do it. They learn that from the adults in the pack, who give them chunks of hide to strip and play with them to teach them the skills they will need for hunting. Once the pups are old enough, they are allowed to accompany the pack on hunting expeditions.

Hunting is wolves' main activity – it's how they get their food. On their leader's initiative, they move out on an expedition, sometimes spending hours and days tracking a good prospect. Wolves usually travel single file behind the leader, which could explain why your dog tends to walk behind you if he's unsure of the destination. After the kill, the immediate goal is to eat and then to rest just enough so the pack can move on again on another outing. Wolves have what are called rendezvous sites, where they know they have a good chance of finding game.

If you watch your dog closely you will be able to see that he has the same sort of pattern, albeit a lot less bloody and exhausting. He has rendezvous sites around your house and yard that he periodically checks for interesting odours. Some dogs have been known to place their toys at these

RIGHT *Small animals like this chipmunk may bring out your dog's natural hunting instincts, even though he probably won't attempt to do more than sniff and maybe chase the prey.*

LEFT *Dogs that are able to spend time outdoors may go through the motions of hunting down and catching prey, but most abandon the chase before it gets this far because they have no real need for the kill.*

The well-trained dog

A well-trained Labrador Retriever waits for permission to move.

Spaniels explore every bit of undergrowth to locate the prey.

Two pointers, having picked up the scent, freeze in the classical pose, nose held high, foreleg lifted, tail an extension of the bodyline.

The good gundog should return swiftly with the prey held very gently in its mouth; the game when released should be unmarked.

Some dogs were specially bred to retrieve the prey from water.

The obedient gundog should relinquish the bird immediately.

LEFT *The hunting instinct is what causes dogs to seek out and try to catch creatures, no matter where they find them.*

RIGHT *It was probably dogs' hunting instinct that led man to domesticate dogs in the first place.*

sites so they will find something there to pick up and play with. And they usually like to eat and then sleep, and are raring to go for a walk or a play session soon after they wake up.

Dogs that are able to spend time outside may even go through the motions of hunting down and catching prey. Just about any dog will gallop after a rabbit or squirrel if given the chance, but most abandon the chase before anything serious occurs.

Unfortunately, some dogs also chase cats because they are small, quick and furry, like other animals of prey. However, a dog living with a cat will probably not try to molest it because it (and all other animals in the house) takes on a sort of "house smell" that ensures an uneventful and peaceful coexistence.

Another manifestation of the hunting instinct may be chasing cars, motorcycles and bikes. Deter your dog by using a leash and jerking him back with a "no" whenever he tries to chase.

Hunting seems very barbaric to those of us who collect our food from the supermarket. It might be difficult to imagine ever feeling quite the same love and trust for Buster if we discovered he had killed a rabbit or bird. Nevertheless, we actually have dogs' hunting instinct to thank for their being in our lives at all, since it was probably their skill at hunting that led man to domesticate dogs in the first place. The dog was better at it than man, so man would follow the tracking dogs and help with the kill. It seemed a fair exchange because man never ate the entire animal and the dog was able to finish off the carcasses that man left behind. Thus, over time, dogs actually got used to man "providing" for them, which led to their viewing man as leader of the pack.

This hunting merger between man and dog still continues today as hunters (now decked in fluorescent orange instead of animal hides) use dogs to help them track and retrieve game. The dog's senses add a lot to man's skills in this area.

DOGS' SUPERIOR SENSES

Man's ears are capable of registering sounds up to 20,000 hertz (waves per second), while a dog hears up to 100,000. That's why a hunting dog will respond to dog whistles at great distances. They are also great at picking out sounds.

Dogs' sense of smell is selective, too. They are able to track the smell of meat through plastic, even distinguishing it from other smells in the same freezer bag. That's also a big advantage when they're trying to sniff out narcotics at an airport or alternatively find a survivor under layers of earthquake rubble.

Dogs can also see very well in dim light because of a special reflective layer at the back of the eyes. Their field of vision (270-plus degrees), also greater than humans, (100), is especially geared toward registering movements.

We tend to overlook sense of touch in dogs, but they have a network of nerves over the entire body to register tactile stimuli and temperature. The most sensitive areas are the nose, paw pads, tongue and lips. Their whiskers (in both snout and eyebrows) are also sensitive.

Comparative vision of dogs and man

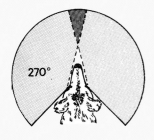

270°

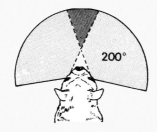

200°

100°

The width of the field of vision is determined by the position of the eyes on the head. Dogs' eyes point to the side to a varying degree, depending on head shape, giving a wide view. Human eyes point forward and are able to focus more clearly.

RIGHT *Hunters now wear orange synthetics instead of animal hides, but the hunting relationship between man and dog still involves the dog's marvellous tracking skills.*

Ultrasonic Hearing

A dog's sense of hearing is in some ways superior to man's.

Independently movable, the ears act as sound shells.

The dog uses one ear to locate the sound source accurately.

Ears prick up to catch a maximum of sound waves.

CHAPTER ELEVEN

Food
glorious food

In the area of feeding, more than in any other area of dog behaviour, the relationship we have established with our dogs is one that makes them remain "puppies". They may look like adult dogs, but like Peter Pan, they never quite take over all the responsibility of being an adult – in this case, finding their own food.

Puppies in the wild are first fed mother's milk and are later fed from the kill by her and the other adult members of the pack. At first the pups cannot chew their own meat, so the adults eat it then regurgitate it, partially digested, for the pups to eat in more liquid form. When the pups are able to chew, they are given pieces by the adults. When they are adults themselves, they will give food to elderly members of the pack as well as the new pack pups.

In our homes, pups are provided for just as they are in the wild. We may not regurgitate, but we teach our pups that all food comes from us and we never allow them to gather their own food. In that sense, they may "feel" like puppies all their lives, which is probably to our advantage because it helps them to see themselves as lower-ranking members of our pack.

Even so, they take an active interest in the provision of that food. Whoever comes in the door with grocery bags is usually greeted in much the same way an adult wolf would be met on coming "home" with a recent kill. While cooking is in progress the dog will take up position in the kitchen just as he would if he were a lower-ranking member of the pack – not allowed to touch the food, but nevertheless waiting for his

BELOW *Domestic dogs remain puppies all their lives in the sense that they are always dependent on the human adults in their packs for food. In the wild, they would have a chance to mature in this manner.*

RIGHT *If two dogs want the same bone, the more dominant dog will be the winner in most situations. Sharing individual, small items is not a natural behaviour among adult dogs.*

turn. This behaviour carries over to the dinner table, where he needs to be if there is a possibility of his getting access to the food.

BEGGING

Begging is a natural extension of this, as it is customary for wolves to "beg" adults for food. Because they are permitted to lick what's left on the adults' lips, don't be surprised if your pooch tends to notice that you have spaghetti sauce on your shirt or a milk moustache. If you allow your dog to beg, you will want to take great care that his breath is good because the idea of begging in the wild is to make sure the adults see you and pay attention to your needs. Your begging dog will do everything possible to make sure he is in your field of vision, even if it means resting his head on the table, breathing on your food, waving his paws at you and bargaining with (temporary) gifts of his toys. (Wolves give sticks and bones in the wild as a submission ritual.)

If your dog's attentive he'll even learn who is and isn't a soft touch and, of those targets, who has to be begged at first because they eat faster than the others. Some dogs won't even rest after you have finished eating. If they know there is food left out anywhere, they beg until it's all gone.

Most people do not appreciate begging, so you might want to deter your dog from doing it. Feed your dog before sitting down to your own meal. Allow him to eat only from his own bowl. Never give him between-meal treats. If your pup needs more to get the message, say "no" when he comes near you to beg. Use a corrective jerk of his leash if necessary.

DIET

You probably won't go wrong feeding your dog commercially prepared foods. Housetraining is more easily regulated in some dogs if they are on dry food, although to avoid allergies and harmful chemicals a natural food is sometimes best.

Most people assume dogs are solely carnivores (meat-eaters) because their wolf ancestors only eat meat. But wolves also eat the partially digested food in the stomach of their herbivorous (plant-eating) prey, which gives them the remaining nutrients they need. A modern diet for the domestic dog may include cereals, rice, vegetables and fruit. Breeders and veterinarians used to recommend a raw egg for a good coat, but in these days of rampant salmonella, raw eggs are not advised. Depending on how active the dog is, the proportion of fat in the diet should be no more than 20–25 per cent.

It's natural for humans to want to respond to dogs' need for food by feeding them whatever and whenever they want – and they will eat as much as they can if they like the food. A healthy adult wolf can eat 20 lb (9 kg) of meat at one feeding. He will also test his powers of swallowing. Adult wolves have been known to "wolf down" an entire caribou tongue in a gulp. However, you're not showing true love for your pet if you're just making him overweight and suscep-

LEFT *Dogs have been known to eat tissues, pebbles, toys, paper and maybe even, in the case of this dog, something that washed up on the beach. He doesn't understand that he does not live in the natural world and may be endangering himself.*

RIGHT *This photograph seems to illustrate how dogs spend approximately 80 per cent of their waking hours, thinking about food, a throwback to wild instincts that tell the dog to always be on the lookout for food sources.*

Hide and seek

If dogs do not eat all their food at once, they frequently cache what is left over; both wild and domestic dogs do this and the most common example of it is the burying of the bone. Any food which is surplus to immediate requirements is likely to be hidden where the dog can easily find it again. Unlike cats, most dogs seem prepared to eat meat that is high almost to the point of rotting.

Foxes will carry the food to be cached to a selected spot.

The food is held in the mouth while a shallow hole is dug.

Soil is replaced over the cache by long sweeps of the nose.

tible to health problems. If your dog is already obese, he needs to be on a strict schedule for feeding and exercise.

Despite the canine reputation for gorging, some dogs act finicky. In highly strung dogs, this may signal a nervous stomach. In dogs bordering on aggressive, it may be a holdout tactic for food they like better – i.e., what is on their owners' plates. Don't let them convince you that they will starve if they don't eat right away – they are well prepared to live off a recent meal for a few days. Wolves can survive up to two weeks without eating.

Don't get caught up in believing your dog is loyal because you feed him, either. Dogs are loyal because you are the leader and offer them companionship, not because you feed them.

No matter what or when you feed your dog, because of his preoccupation with food he will probably be unable to resist food odours from your rubbish bin unless you have trained him that rooting through the rubbish displeases you.

Another unattractive habit your dog may have is eating faeces or his own vomit. Although it's disgusting to humans, for dogs it's a survival instinct. In the den, the mother licks up her pups' waste, just as she ate the afterbirth when they were born. Removing any traces of them ensures their protection from predators. However, along with being an unacceptable habit in a human household, it also puts the dog in danger of picking up parasites from another animal.

Dogs have also been known to eat tissues, pebbles, toys and paper. If a trend develops, have a veterinarian check your dog out because the need to eat strange objects could be the result of an enzyme deficiency.

Dogs also have a habit of burying bones and leftover food as a carryover from when their species needed to do this to store food for later. Although our domesticated canines are rarely in danger of starvation, they have been unable to shed this instinct and might end up digging in your garden to follow it.

CHAPTER TWELVE

The pleasures of play

You've probably seen a comic sketch on television in which a man goes to a woman's highrise apartment to pick her up for a date and finds himself waiting in the living room by himself for a few minutes before his companion for the evening is ready.

Her dog enters the room with a ball and entices the visitor into playing a few rounds of "fetch". But one throw – the last – manages to bounce out on to the balcony and over the railing. And the dog, always a trooper, takes a flying leap over the rail to go after it, presumably only to come to a squashed ending on the ground quite a few floors below.

The joke usually ends with the man being relieved to know that the dog landed safely and softly on an awning. The fact that the dog actually put himself in such dire danger to catch that ball is a little farfetched. But for a second, those of us who have played with dogs believed this nightmarish scenario could have happened.

In the wild wolf packs, play is a daily occurrence among most members of the pack. Pups play with each other almost from the day they can move, rolling and tumbling together, and later chasing and fighting over objects. Play serves as a training tool, sharpening their skills, reactions and interpretation of each other's signals. This

ABOVE *Puppies play with each other from the moment they can move, rolling and tumbling together and later chasing and fighting over objects. This teaches them skills they would later need in the wild.*

Play with other dogs

The dog may assume different poses during the course of the game, from the classic bow soliciting play to others indicating submission.

Tugging the other dog's tail to elicit a playful response.

LEFT *Because this dog likes his child master on the opposite haystack, he'll do everything he can to jump over to him during play. Many dogs retain play characteristics into old age.*

To initiate play with a smaller dog, the naturally dominant larger one will often roll on his back, assuming a submissive posture.

Tempting behaviour: the opponent is offered the ball.

keeps them safe in the wild and serves to teach them good hunting tactics. Wolves play all their lives, even into old age, because they take on the responsibility of teaching the young. Play also serves to keep them fit and hones their own hunting skills between kills.

Since dogs, especially those who live in cities, have little chance for hunting and even socializa-tion with other dogs, it's up to us to fulfil their need to play, as well as to exercise them and keep them amused and happy.

If you throw a ball, chances are your dog is going to run after it, leap on it as it if were prey and carry it around for a while. It may take some training for him to learn you want him to give it back so you can repeat the exercise, but most dogs will gladly bear with you as you try this. Don't be too hard on him if it takes longer than you expected it to – the purpose here is fun for both owner and animal, not perfection.

Using toys to play with the dog will make him associate the toys with pleasant times with you. If you give him the toys when you go out he won't be as lonely, and he'll probably be prone to playing on his own.

GAMES TO PLAY

Besides "fetch", there are a few other games you might want to teach your dog:

Tug It's a natural instinct for your dog not to want to give up something he's got in his mouth, so he's a prime candidate for tugging. Gently pull on the other side of his ball, making sure he understands you are not threatening him. It's

LEFT *Play serves to keep adult dogs fit and hone their "hunting" skills. Even though dogs no longer have a real need to hunt, the instinct to play remains.*

RIGHT *Dogs in cities have little chance to play like this dog and boy, so they need more exercise to keep them happy and amused.*

best if you've already taught him "release". (See Chapter Six)

Hide and Seek Get him involved in a chase session and then run ahead of him from room to room, hiding behind the door or some other piece of furniture (or under a blanket) for him to find you.

Blanket chase Hold an object under a blanket you don't mind the dog sinking his teeth into. Move it around and encourage the dog to play-chase and even catch it through the blanket. Brave people or those wearing gloves can dispense with the blanket.

Which hand? Hold a small object (or even food) in one of your hands and let the dog poke at the hand he thinks it's in. Repetition is really fun with this one.

Monkey (dog) in the middle Two people throw a ball across the room with the dog seated on the floor between them, trying to catch the ball as it passes overhead. It's best if the dog can sit a little behind the line of throw so he doesn't do a back flip as he jumps to intercept.

Hide the toy Show him a toy and then hide it under something like a pillow and tell him to get the toy.

Catch The dog sits on the floor and catches his ball in his jaws when it is thrown to him. Then he walks it back and is told to back up so play can continue.

Stairs catch Standing at the bottom of a flight of enclosed stairs, throw the ball to the dog, who is standing at the top, waiting to catch it. Then encourage the dog to roll the ball down the stairs.

LEFT *Timber's head is visible at the top of the stairs as he waits for someone to take him up on his invitation to play a game of ball on the stairs. It has become a ritual in the authors' home.*

CHAPTER THIRTEEN
Trespassers beware

Maybe your dog barks at the car in the next lane in the intersection. Maybe he walks around with a particular toy that he doesn't want a child to have. Maybe he's decided that no other dogs should walk on the pavement in front of your house.

Whatever the particular symptom, the diagnosis is probably territoriality. Territory is defined as the area an animal will defend against members of the same species. In the case of domesticated dogs, because they live with humans, they may consider humans to be the same species.

Protecting the home and family from intruders is a basic instinct for dogs. It's not always a very useful one any more. The number of times you really need a dog to be territorial are few compared to the times he does it for some reason that seems silly to you.

LEFT *Even though it is sometimes not very useful, it is a natural instinct for a dog to see your home and family as his territory and to protect it when he feels it is necessary.*

RIGHT *Bonding is a necessary first step in effectively training your dog. When she is secure and confident, she will be happy to approach and learn from you, her leader.*

Communication by scent

When a dog scratches the ground with his hind legs, he probably leaves an odour from the sweat glands in his toes and foot pads.

Dogs have a tendency to roll in foul-smelling substances, so that the strong smell will command respect from other dogs.

An adult male will mark out his territory by urinating on trees and lamp posts, causing other dogs to mark and claim the same areas.

The immature male adopts this position while urinating.

The female does not lift her hind leg but squats.

Wolf packs have territories of over 100 miles (160 km), so is it any wonder that our dogs bark when someone approaches the pavement right in front of the house, let alone dares to step on the front porch?

If you, the leader of this pack, accept the stranger, the dog will probably also accept him. After all, the defence of the pack is your res-

ponsibility. But if the dog sees that you are afraid or angry, he may join in to back you up.

Visitors who come and go very quickly reinforce the dog's impulse to bark. The dog barks, they leave, the dog feels that he has been successful and will bark the next time.

Be careful you don't give a dog the wrong signal when you're trying to correct him from

defending his territory. If you pull him back and comfort him, he may think you are thanking him for protecting you.

Dogs mark their territory by leaving their own scent with faeces and urine. That's why they urinate so often when you take them outside. They also spend a lot of time sniffing to see who else has been there and to know where to place their own scent to mask earlier ones. Another form of scent-marking is scraping the ground with the hind paws, which also releases scent from the sweat glands there.

Female dogs are not quite as interested as males are in leaving and reading scents. Only just before and during their heat period (oestrus) do they show increased interest in male markings. They have no territory of their own to mark, so they can squat instead of raising a leg.

When a dog defecates, he will probably sniff the faeces to be sure he has left his scent. (The

ABOVE *Territory doesn't seem so important to this beagle, who is allowing a hen to be among her young puppies. She probably came to know the hen as part of the "pack" long before the puppies were born.*

RIGHT *A doberman and a husky fight it out for the territory along this beach, displaying the need for dogs to discover who ranks higher and to have dominion over certain areas.*

dog probably thinks defecating is especially good because, in addition to the fact that it marks his territory, you usually praise him for doing it.)

INTRODUCING ANOTHER PET

If you want to add a second dog to your household, be aware that both dogs will have to assert themselves to see who comes out top dog. If the newcomer is still a puppy, there may be no contest – the older dog will win out on seniority alone. If you are combining two bitches, though, you may have your hands full. It is best to get

them both from the same litter because litter mates usually get along well together.

If you have pets of another species – cat, bird, ferret – a new puppy will probably adjust well to them. An older dog, however, will call for more caution. Do not force things – let them approach each other gradually under supervision. If the pets are natural prey of canines – hamsters, guinea pigs, rabbits – keep them in their cages and do not let them out when the dog is in the room.

FIGHTING

If your dog meets up with another dog, there will be an instinctive need to defend territory or establish rank, even if there is no real dog pack involved. The possibility of a fight is even greater if one dog enters another's yard or home. A dog on a leash will fight another dog to assert territorial rights to the person at the end of the leash.

Dogs that have never been socialized with other dogs are likely candidates for fighting. Some fight because they were attacked by another dog when they were puppies.

If your dog is on a leash during a fight, jerk the leash, say "heel" and walk in the opposite direction. If he's not on a leash, pull him up by the tail. Do not go near the dogs' faces. As a last-ditch deterrent, you might try throwing an object near them, throwing a blanket over one of them or spraying them with water.

If you have failed in your attempts to prevent the fight, the dogs' hackles are raised, and they are trying to appear larger by standing sideways or lowering their heads, get as far out of their way as possible.

Aggression

This behaviour on meeting is frequently seen in wolves and dogs. The dogs face each other, tails stiffly outstretched, lips retracted.

The inferior dog will then adopt a crouching position, lowering its tail and flattening its ears.

Squatting on the ground, the submissive dog will try to lick the other's muzzle. The dominant dog stands, its ears and tail erect.

If the dominant dog continues to show aggression, the subordinate one lies on its back and shows its genital organs in total submission.

CHAPTER FOURTEEN

The technological dog

omestic dogs are no longer in a wild land, where they could hunt and kill and play on their own terms. They are in our land, where technology has taken over and even we humans are far from our original natural surroundings.

It's been said that the difference between animals and humans is that animals don't have the power to reason but even though dogs can't reason, they can get used to our human world, and even come to expect certain things. Sometimes, however, they can't know what to expect, and when they react with fear and excitement, they're labelled out of control.

It might help them if we could understand just what they think about some of the technology we have come to take for granted, so this section

LEFT *There are places in the kitchen dogs should learn to stay away from, even when they smell food odours that prey on their endless search for food.*

RIGHT *Peanuts has overcome his fear of kids' vehicles and has even learned to ride along with his friend. Activities like this can become welcome rituals in a dog's life.*

is a glossary of terms based on what we think our dog would say (if he could) about his world. Maybe it will help you comprehend the world that your dog is dealing with.

Because dogs spent about 80 per cent of their waking hours (we won't get into how many hours that actually is, for those who already resent dogs' lives of leisure) thinking about eating, the tour starts in the kitchen.

Refrigerator This is where the more dominant members of my pack (my owners) put the kill when they bring home food for the pack. They never ask me to partake in the hunt, but I like to watch this storing away part because there are lots of good smells that are taken out of bags and put into this big cold box. Because of this, we never have to worry about where we buried our food for later.

Waste disposal and dishwasher Very loud, will probably hurt you if you get too close because it sounds as if there's a lot of banging going on. There are a few other things in the kitchen that make a lot of noise, too, usually high, shrill noises that really hurt my ears.

Microwave oven The bell goes off and, soon after, we eat. I like this oven because I can hang around and watch my owners cook while this one is on. When they're using the big one with the big door that opens out over the floor, I'm constantly being told to move out of the way, and the kitchen gets very hot.

Vacuum cleaner This is so dangerous they keep it in a closet, and when they get it out, it attacks you and tries to suck you up. Speaking of cleaning, I really hate it when they spray that stuff on the

glass coffee table – I walk around it coughing so they know I hate it instead of just leaving the room where it won't bother me.

Television Other animals get into the house through this noisy box in ways that prevent me from hearing or smelling their approach. Usually it's just other people, but sometimes a barking dog, a howling wolf or a chattering monkey will come in, and I'll have to chase it away.

Sometimes they don't even make a noise, and I can't ever smell them, but I can see the outline of their bodies and get to them just in time. And sometimes I'll get to chase a bird or respond to a baby crying or someone giggling.

The television lets me know that my owners have finally given in to my proddings for bedtime. Along with the lights, this is usually turned off during that busy time of night when I'm doing my bedtime ritual: going out for the last time, eating a few nuggets of food to last me through the night and finding a favourite toy to take with me to the den.

Telephone This doesn't bother me too much because I'm used to the ringing. But sometimes I think my owners are talking to me and then when I look, I see that they're holding this thing at their heads. I guess it's a comfort thing or maybe a game for them.

Computers I'm not sure what they do at these. They sit in front of them for hours and you hear tap, tap, tap and maybe a beep once in a while, or paper spews forth. I know they love the things, so sometimes I have to go and sit underneath them and put my face in their laps to let them know I need a hug or a trip outside or that it's time to go to bed.

Bathtub My owners go in here every morning to get away from me I think. They tell me it's OK for me to come in the room, but they know I don't like to go in there when the water's running because that's what happens when they take me to have a bath. On the other hand, there are lots of interesting smells in that room, so I don't mind going in there when nobody's in the tub.

RIGHT *When you are on the telephone, dogs are sometimes unsure if you are talking to them or to somebody else. Most of them won't understand if you hold the phone up to their ear to hear the caller, either.*

RIGHT *The bathroom has a lot of great smells in it, but the dog may not enjoy going in there when you have decided it's time for his regular bath.*

OPPOSITE LEFT *Dogs who have to get used to hearing other animals on television probably see the dogs on television as actually alive, coming out of the set into their territory.*

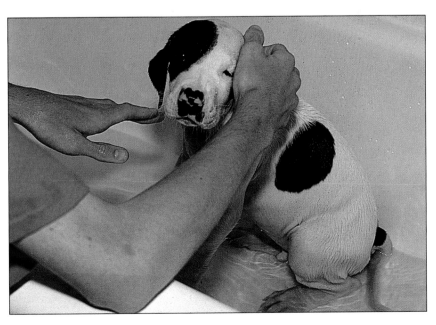

Alarm clock When this goes off in the morning, they hit it and lie down again. I'm glad it's not me making that awful noise or they'd hit me, too. The alarm means it's OK for me to crawl up from the bottom of the bed and kiss them.

Doors Parts of the wall that open, and great smells abound on the other side. Sometimes the doors that are inside the house shut me out from my favourite toys or keep me from the pack for something they call "privacy".

Doorbell A ding I hear whenever I already know that someone is on the porch. Sometimes, though, I hear the bell and there's no one there. Usually I'm told that it was "just the TV".

BELOW *Unusually high sounds inaudible to the human ear can emanate from television sets and other electronic appliances, so be sure your dog is not feeling any discomfort when you use these.*

RIGHT *Your dog doesn't know how doors work or why you need them, but he knows that he usually can't get through them without your being there to open them for him.*

Car We get into this when we go for a "ride". I always have to sit in the back in a harness. I don't like to put my head out of the window because particles fly through the air into my face and my nose dries up. But in warm weather I do like to be at the receiving end of the cool air vents.

Sometimes we just end up at a 7-Eleven or a petrol station, and all I get to do is sit in the car (not on really hot or really cold days) and maybe bark at some people who pull in right next to us.

Parks or peoples' houses are other destinations. The park usually involves a lot of natural smells, lots of running and maybe chasing squirrels (just far enough to make it fun) and a wade or swim through a stream to fetch a stick.

The peoples' house usually involves good food smells, some new faces to kiss, some new hands to pet me, some new socks to make an attempt at and maybe some kids to play with. But watch out for those bikes and be sure you don't go out of range when you get caught up in running with the kids (because you get corrected even if they don't). I don't think that's always fair.

Unfortunately, about twice a year the ride ends up at the local veterinary clinic. There's a cold metal table and a few nice women who don't seem to want to hurt me but always do in one way or another. I really hate all that poking and prodding all over my body.

Expect to be really tired when you come back from any of these places – rides are exhausting no matter where they end up because you have to be so "on" not to miss anything or because there's a lot of anxiety attached to getting out of the den.

Assorted Technology Sometimes I get a little anxious around technology, so it's up to my owners to be more careful. I don't really know what I'm dealing with here, so they have to be sure I don't get tangled in cords or become too startled.

Unusual sounds and frequencies inaudible to humans can come from TV sets and other appliances. If my owners see me tilting my head in a strange way, they check to see if what they're using is hurting my ears.

ABOVE *If your dog likes to ride in the car, he'll probably enjoy going with you just about anywhere and can even be trained to learn the names of some destinations.*

CHAPTER FIFTEEN

I'm not always a hero

It's your puppy's first summer, and because of the season a thunderstorm is brewing. Suddenly the skies open, and at the sound of the first loud crack, your dog suddenly runs from the other room and jumps into your lap, quivering, displaying very submissive behaviour. He looks pleadingly into your eyes, asking openly for your protection from whatever is making that awful banging noise.

Noise is one of many things that can cause your dog to react pitifully. Stairs, vacuum cleaners, the dark, strange moving objects and

LEFT *Noise, stairs, vacuum cleaners, the dark, strange moving objects and just about anything he's unsure of can make a dog cringe and turn to you for comfort.*

RIGHT *If it's an object your dog is afraid of, but something you feel he can deal with, give him time to adjust and then let him approach the object if he wants to. If he can handle it, he'll do his best to get used to it.*

just about anything he's unsure of can make him cringe and turn to you for comfort. Sickness can also make him feel he needs you because he perceives it, too, as an outside threat. Sometimes just the trip to the veterinarian is worse than the sickness itself.

Some dogs react to fear by biting, in a manner different from the biting of overly aggressive dogs. They bite in what they perceive as self-defence, even when there is no actual danger. This is usually caused by failure at socialization early in life and may be overcome over time by good training.

If the menace is an object – something your dog can deal with – it may help to give him time to adjust and then let him approach the object voluntarily when the time is right for him.

Temporarily captive wild wolves have been observed reacting to people who enter the enclosure. First, the wolf tries to paw himself out, jumps into the air, then retreats into the farthest corner, crouching, cowering, panting, trembling, salivating, defecating and urinating.

Then the wolf relaxes, unless the person moves. Later he allows the person to approach and touch him. Soon after the wolf begins to approach the person, chewing his clothing, rubbing him, rolling in his scent.

Finally, when the wolf is sure he is no longer threatened, he wags his tail, approaches the person without aggression and greets with the mouth wolf greeting.

Maybe it's a kid's motorized car or walking doll that frightens your dog. Following the wolf

procedure, it's safe to say your dog will at first get as far away from it as possible, or he might choose the safety of your protective arms even if you are closer to the object than the farthest corner. He may do some whining, but if he's not trapped (don't try to trap him), he probably won't act much more submissive.

Keep the toy quiet at first, giving the dog a chance to get used to it from afar. Eventually the dog will calm a little, and if you accompany him, he will probably approach the toy – but give him a chance to decide when and if he's ready to do it. Pushing him into it won't accomplish the goal.

Once he gets close enough to the toy, he will sniff it and maybe even touch it, and then will probably feel quite pleased with himself that he has overcome this obstacle.

If the menace is a noise, or something else the dog cannot get close to, all you can do is to calm him by letting him know you will take care of him. Tell him it's OK, that he's a good boy, and talk him through it. If nothing else, it will distract him from the noise.

Some dogs are fearful of cars and need to be desensitized gradually. Do not make him feel trapped in the car. Chances are he was traumatized by being confined in some enclosed space, or he could have had a bad experience in a car – an accident, a backfire, horns, harassment.

His problem could also be car sickness, which manifests itself with vomiting or otherwise messing the car. Do not feed or water him before a trip, and be careful about jostling him around. Most dogs would prefer to be confined in a crate or held fast with a doggy seat belt rather than be constantly sliding across the seat.

If he does mess in the car, as well as in the house, he may react like a "bad dog". Reassure him that he is a good dog so he doesn't feel that he has to be punished.

If the veterinarian needs to examine him, be prepared for a lot of clinging. There's no way around this. Reward him for going through it all.

Some puppies are afraid of stairs, especially open tread ones that allow you to see the ground below the steps. If you guide him and make sure he knows he has your support, through touch and soothing talk, he will be willing to give it a try for you. Be sure the pup is physically large enough to handle stairs before you force him into it. More than one pup has taken a tumble down a few steps because his front legs didn't make it to the lower step before his rump got too heavy.

Other people may frighten your dog. This is not unexpected, for wolf pups become apprehensive about strange individuals at three months. This, too, can be overcome with habitude. Whatever the fear, do not make it worse by comforting the dog too much. Sometimes a "no" or "enough" will snap the dog out of it. Be sure to praise a good response to something the dog used to run from.

LEFT *Dogs perceive illness as an outside threat, so if your dog is sick he will need you to be there to comfort him.*

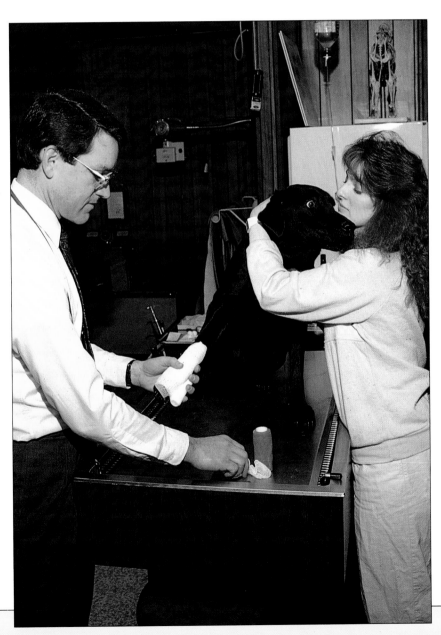

RIGHT *Sometimes the trip to the veterinarian is worse than the illness itself. Expect a lot of clinging.*

CHAPTER SIXTEEN

My dog is not a lunatic

Now you've read this book, you probably understand a good deal more about your dog's behaviour. You now realize that what you thought was odd was in fact your dog just acting like a dog. To review what that means:

A dog who follows you wherever you go (even to the bathroom) is just being a good pack animal, following your lead, hanging around to see what you want him to do next.

Turning around in circles before napping is a habit that dates back to the dog's wild ancestors, who had to stamp down the grass to form a hollow to settle into. It also aids the curving of the spine necessary for the typical curled-up pose he plans to get into.

A dog who mounts your visitors may be feeling a little more dominant or aggressive than you would like.

If a dog loves the husband but hates the wife, it may be because he sees the husband as leader of the pack and feels he has to compete with the wife for the No. 2 spot.

Defending a certain member of your family, perhaps a child, may mean he sees that person as a younger member of the pack, a puppy unable as yet to fend for itself.

Stealing socks and underwear may seem like an offence. But your dog does it only to get your attention or to comfort himself if he's feeling a little uncomfortable.

LEFT *This dog is practically climbing the walls to be part of the pack — a natural instinct, not odd behaviour.*

LEFT *Like wolves in the wild that depend on each other for everything, this dog is depending on his owner to carry him for the rest of the hike.*

RIGHT *This basset hound pup has got himself into a situation he can't get out of. Odd behaviour or natural instinct to play?*

Barking at a cat on television is a natural re-action for the dogs territorial instincts. The dog doesn't know the cat is only a picture and believes it is actually intruding on his territory.

Waking up the other members of the pack by licking is pretty much the job of the one who wakes up first. That's why your dog seems to love you so much in the morning.

Since the dog has been programmed genetically to be wary of anyone other than the familiar, he seems to display great fear of, or animosity toward, the postman.

Your dog's ball (or other toy) is most precious to him, so when he drops it at your feet or pushes it on to your lap as a way of begging, he feels he is offering you a wonderful token of submission or a really good trade.

Wild wolf pups are known to beg by licking the lips of the adults. That's why your dog thinks it's OK to be what humans consider offensive in his never-ending quest for food.

Sniffing crotches, although not desirable to you, is a direct carryover from dog society where sniff-ing private areas determines who has higher rank.

Dogs like to smell doggy, so rolling in things like manure that contribute to his own individual doggy smell is a real upper for your pooch. Don't expect him to enjoy the bath you're going to insist on. He worked hard for that particular scent blend and is not keen to be rid of it.

Wolves in the wild depend on each other for everything – they hunt, eat, sleep, play and raise families together. To be sent away from all that is to lose life as they know it and they are not sure how to cope. That's why your dog cries and whines when you lock him in a separate room.

Picking fights with other dogs is a last-ditch way to determine who's a higher-ranking dog. If knowing that is important to your dog, he'll probably try to fight or at least do the dance that leads up to one to sort it out.

So now you see that there really is nothing wrong with your dog – at least nothing that probably can't be fixed with some work.

If you discovered while reading that your dog is not OK because of something you did along the way, it won't do any good to blame yourself and feel guilty. Now that you know the problem, you can work with your dog to find a solution. And if you're just embarking on puppy-raising, your new knowledge will provide the basis for a good start for both of you.

You now know that you have to treat your dog like a dog and make him think you're acting like a dog – the lead dog. Both you and your dog are going to be OK.

ABOVE *Motorcycle riding may not be on the top of your dog's activity list, but running around sniffing and thinking about food probably are.*

LEFT *Because your dog looks on you as the leader of his pack, he will probably attempt to do anything you want him to, even rafting.*

RIGHT *Your dog's toys help make him feel secure in his surroundings, so when he drops them at your feet he is giving you a wonderful token of submission.*

Index

abuse 39, 52
actions, human 52
activities 65
affection 15, 57
aggressive behaviour 44, 45, 57, 91–3, 122
  attack 52
  communication 50
  food 108
  growling 39
  leash behaviour 50, 51
  mounting 94, 137
  see also dominant behaviour
alarm clocks 128
alertness 42, 44
allergies 105
antagonism toward children 30
anxiety 79, 80
approval 18
arousal 44
assertive behaviour 34
atmosphere sensitivity 24
attachment 23
  response 82
  to objects 81
attack 42
  aggressive behaviour 52
attention
  lack of 33
  seeking 137
  span 57
authority in posture 52

babies and dogs 31–3
baby-talk *see* high-pitched voice
bait 96
barking 38, 39, 77, 78–9, 93, 139
  visitors 119
basset hound 139
baths 127, 140
beagle 120
begging 105, 139
  gesture 45
behaviour 111, 136–41
  acceptable 7
  domestic 8
  natural 105
  problems 77, 87
  rituals 17–21
  submissive 11
bell conditioning 87, 88
bikes, chasing of 100
biological clocks 18
bisexual nature 95
biting 15, 77, 93
  reaction to fear 133
body language 42–5, 50–2

body posture and submissive behaviour 71
bonding 26, 27–30, 31, 50, 56, 117
  children and dogs 30
  positive 52
bones
  burying 108
  poultry 106
border collies 87
boredom 79
breeders 106
brushing 92, 93
burying 12

cache 108
Canidae 12
cars 129, 130
  chasing 100
  fear 134
  sickness 134
catching 114
  prey 100
cats 100, 119, 122, 139
cereals 106
Certificate of Pedigree 15
chasing 95, 114
  cars 100
  cats 100
  prey 72, 99, 100
chemicals, harmful 105
chewing 77, 79
  pups 73
chihuahua 11
child substitute 26
children 14
  and dogs 30–1
  dogs level 29
  fear 92
circling 137
city dogs 113
classic bow 111
classical conditioning 87
coat condition 106
coexistence with other pets 119, 120–2
collars 56, 62, 64, 65
collies, border 87
"come" command 56, 60, 62, 87
comfort 24, 25
  seeking 137
commands 48, 49, 50, 52, 53–69
  attentiveness 73
  defiance 39
  lack of response 71
  obedience 81
  potential for learning 54
  understanding 49
  training 62

vocal 78
  words/actions 55
  see also voice commands
communication 41, 44, 50
  facial expression 43
  by scent 118
computers 127
conditioning 87
confinement 71
contentment 42
correction 50, 52, 56, 74, 92
coyote 12
cropping 44
crouching position 122

dachshund 42
Darwin, Charles 12
deep tone voice 50
defecation *see* faeces
defence
  family 137
  territory 120, 122
defiance 39
dependence 23, 26, 138
  on humans 104
deterrents, furniture trespassing 82
diet 105–8
discipline 15, 74, 80
  wolf 72
disease 45
dishwasher 125
dislike of dogs 89–96
disobedience 10
display behaviour 21
distraction 57, 58
distress, severe 87
doberman 121
docking 42, 44
domestic behaviour 8
domestic dog 12
domestication of dogs 100, 101, 124
dominance games 74
dominant behaviour 11, 34, 35, 45, 122
with children 31, 32
  children and fear 92
  facial expression 42
  food 105
  greeting 45
  illness 34
  mounting 94, 137
  pack 32
  running away 95
dominant male 11
doorbells 128
doors 37, 128, 129
"down" command 87
  see also "lie down"

command
dry food 105

ears 42
eating and growling 91
eggs 106
electronic appliances 128
emotions, owner 82
"enough" command 135
environment 39
enzyme deficiency 108
excitement 39, 42, 44, 90, 124
exclusion 71
exercise 48, 113
  routines 20
experience 29
eye contact 45, 52

facial contact 52
facial expressions 42, 43
faeces 120
  eating 108
family
  defence 137
  protection 116, 119
fat 106
fear 42, 44, 79, 124, 125, 131–5
  children 92
  of dogs 91
  people 93
fearful aggression 44
feeding 18, 29, 52
  amount 106
  regularity 106
  time 87, 88
female
  subpack 11
  unspayed 80
"fetch" command 66, 113
fighting 21, 34, 78, 121, 122, 141
films 50, 85
firm tone/voice 52, 56
fitness 112
following 137
food 34, 103–8, 124
  hiding 108
  reward 68
  tips 106
  wild instincts 106, 107
  see also feeding
Form of Transfer 15
foxes 108
frequencies 129
fruit 106
furniture 82, 93

games 113–14
genetic background 87

Picture Credits

Betts Anderson/Unicorn Stock Photographs: pp47, 124. Walt Anderson/Visuals Unlimited: p138. W. Banaszewski/Visuals Unlimited: p41. Steve Bourgeois/Unicorn Stock Photographs: p127T. Kimberley Burnham/Unicorn Stock Photographs: p116. Deneve Feigh Bunde/Unicorn Stock Photographs: pp105, 139, 140. Diane Calkins/Click the Photo Connection: pp6, 10, 13T, 16, 19, 23, 25, 29, 33, 37, 49, 56, 62B, 74, 80, 86T, 88, 93, 100, 106, 118, 134, 137. D. Cavagnaro/Visuals Unlimited: p7. John D. Cunningham/Visuals Unlimited: p117. Kent and Donna Dannen: pp1, 2, 28, 38, 39, 40, 64, 85, 90. Gail Denham: pp81, 126, 141. Joel Dexter/Unicorn Stock Photographs: p120. Eugene L. Drifmeyer/Photri Inc.: p125. John Ebeling/Unicorn Stock Photographs: p54. Margaret Finefrock/Unicorn Stock Photographs: p113. Rod Furgason/Unicorn Stock Photographs: p127B. Bruce Gaylord/Visuals Unlimited: p141T. Michael and Elvan Habicht/Photri Inc.: p63. James A. Hays/Unicorn Stock Photographs: p51. Arthur R. Hill/Visuals Unlimited: pp20, 96. Linda H. Hopson/Visuals Unlimited: pp57, 119. Tom Huggler/Outdoor Images: p73T.

Bo Jarner/Photri Inc.: p101. Arnie Katz/Unicorn Stock Photographs: p24. B. Kinney: pp98, 110. Rubin Klaas: p66. B. Kulik/Photri Inc.: 13B. Lani/Photri Inc.: pp21, 91. Dave Lyons/Unicorn Stock Photographs: p121. Joe McDonald/Visuals Unlimited: p18. Paul Murphy/Unicorn Stock Photographs: pp34, 132. Perry Murphy/Unicorn Stock Photographs: p62T, 71, 73B. David Newman/Visuals Unlimited: p86B. Photri Inc.: pp11, 15, 31, 32, 44, 68, 92, 95, 99, 107, 129. Frank Sanborne: pp26, 43. Lisa Sardan/Photri Inc.: p14B. Chuck Schmeiser/Unicorn Stock Photographs: p102. Marcus Schneck; p114. Rosemary Shelton: pp14T, 27, 30, 50, 52, 60, 82, 94, 104, 128, 133. Jim Shippee/Unicorn Stock Photographs: pp72, 135. Larry Stanley/Unicorn Stock Photographs: p79. H. H. Thomas III/Unicorn Stock Photographs: pp8, 77. Dave Underwood/Click the Photo Connection: p69. Les Van/Unicorn Stock Photographs: p67. Aneal Vohra/Unicorn Stock Photographs: pp112, 130. Dick Young/Unicorn Stock Photographs: p111.